Frank's Arms

Stories & Lessons from a Caregiver and Patient Advocate

Deborah L. Phelps, Ph.D.

Frank's Arms
Stories & Lessons from a Caregiver and Patient Advocate

© 2015 by Deborah L. Phelps, Ph.D.

ISBN: 978-1-63110-139-7

Library of Congress Control Number: 2015919382

All Rights Reserved Under
International and Pan-American Copyright Conventions.
No part of this book may be used or reproduced in any manner whatsoever without written permission except in the case of brief quotations embodied in critical articles or reviews.

Cover Illustration: Armback by Kurt Perschke

Printed in the United States of America by
Mira Digital Publishing
Chesterfield, Missouri 63005

Dedication

*I dedicate this memoir to Frank
and to all caregivers and widows*

Frank's Arms:

Contents

iii Dedication
vii Preface

Part One Background
    3 Introduction
    9 Frank's Illness
  15 My Gift to Frank
  19 Taking Care of Myself

Part Two Medical Interventions
  29 Three Months to Live
  33 Gallbladder Surgery
  39 Infected Stitch
  43 Beginning of the End
  47 Feeding Tube Removal
  51 Do Not Resuscitate
  57 Comfort
  61 Death's Dress Rehearsal
  65 Death

Part Three Widowhood
  73 Funeral
  79 My Deal with Frank
  85 New Role as Widow
  93 Avenues for Escape
103 Transition into Singlehood
105 Conclusion

Part Four REFLECTIONS
109 Things I Wish I Had Known
113 Other Caregiving Insights
117 Epilogue

119 Glossary
133 References
137 Acknowledgments
141 About the Author

Preface

On the following pages, I share stories and lessons learned from seven years of caregiving and advocacy for my husband, Frank, during his battle with scleroderma, an incurable autoimmune disorder.

When I began my role as Frank's caregiver and advocate in 1997, I held a doctorate in medical sociology, which is the study of systems and social behavior in the medical field, including the patient-physician relationship. The degree did not qualify me as a medical professional, but my education background helped me in two ways. First, I understood the politics in medical organizations. Second, I had the confidence to challenge Frank's providers to ensure he received the care we thought he needed. I learned to question medicine and to "peel the onion" to reveal the dynamics of Frank's health care. Day after day, I remembered sociology tenets from Peter Berger in *Invitation to Sociology* (1963):

> *"...the first wisdom of sociology is this: things are not what they seem. Social reality turns out to have many layers of meaning. The discovery of each new layer changes the perception of the whole. There is a debunking motif inherent in sociological consciousness."*

As a student, I developed critical and independent thinking skills and embraced Berger's points and also the ideas of multiple perspectives related to social issues and multiple ways to solve problems. I was a healthy skeptic in general; as such, I was prepared to be a creative advocate during Frank's treatment and hospital stays. I tended not to take "no" for an answer in my role as his advocate.

In addition, I am an expert in emotional detachment, which stemmed from my childhood relationships with my family. This served me well during Frank's illness when I had to challenge the medical professionals. I came across a quote from *Invisible* (2014), a James Patterson novel that sums up my state of mind during the progression of his disease and death:

> "I'm a girl standing in a tornado, pretending like it isn't even windy, like I can compartmentalize every emotion, switch off my heart and divert every ounce of my energy into my brain..."

However, compartmentalizing my emotions took its toll on me. When Frank's struggle with scleroderma ended, and I was no longer his caregiver and advocate, I focused on myself spiritually and emotionally in ways I had been unable to do while Frank was ill.

Some of the following chapters are stories about medical interventions during the later stages of Frank's disease, told in a loosely chronological order with reflections and lessons learned included in Part II. I had planned to focus primarily on my caregiving and advocacy experiences, but I realized my strategies in coping as a widow were important aspects of my journey. I also share my shifts in self-identity and consciousness from a newly widowed woman into singlehood.

Other lessons that I learned are sprinkled throughout the book, some of which I wish I had recognized and anticipated sooner. I hope you will relate to the challenges and opportunities for growth I reflect upon in my memoir and will gain insight into your own experiences. Coping mechanisms are as varied as people and their unique journeys; no one universal path exists for coping with caregiving or grief. I encourage you to embrace and discover what works best for you.

Ultimately, this book is about Frank's influence on me. Frank's arms have been wrapped around me throughout our marriage, his illness and death, in widowhood, and even in my transition to singlehood. Though I supported him as his caregiver, he supported me throughout our relationship, in graduate school, in my academic career, and as my companion all along the way. His arms were the second parts of his body to be affected by scleroderma. He controlled his illness through me as I became an extension of him. Even though Frank died years ago, he still has an impact on me as I make my way through the challenges of life without him.

Frank was a role model for hard work, perseverance, and positive thinking. In responding to these characteristics, I was happy to reflect them back to him during his illness. At the same time, Frank loved me unconditionally. He witnessed my life and struggles with a belief in me that never wavered.

I'm struck by the relevance to a scene from a movie, *Shall We Dance* (2004), with Susan Sarandon and Richard

Deborah L. Phelps, Ph.D.

Gere. Susan Sarandon's character, Beverly Clark, talked about the point of marriage:

> *"We need a witness to our lives. There's a billion people on the planet ... I mean, what does anyone life really mean? But in a marriage, you're promising to care about everything... You're saying, 'Your life will not go unnoticed because I will notice it.'..."*

Frank and I were meant to team up as a couple. I was his witness and here is part of our story.

PART ONE

BACKGROUND

Introduction

FRANK WAS LOOKING FOR COMPANIONSHIP and so was I when I lifted my head from my textbook.

One night in 1984 while deeply engrossed in doing my sociology homework, I realized my stomach was growling, but I wanted to keep working. I knew my friend, Rich, was about to end his shift as the supervisor at an aluminum company and hoped he could pick up a burger for me on his way home. He was busy, but he asked his co-worker, Frank, to take his place. Rich, knowing I needed a break, gave Frank ten dollars to take me to a restaurant.

I suspect Rich had matchmaking in mind.

I lived in an efficiency basement unit in the trendy Central West End (CWE) in Saint Louis, Missouri. The CWE was a vibrant neighborhood filled with small restaurants, unique clothing stores, boutiques, and antique shops. Frank and I shared our first meal at Dressel's, a Welsh pub that catered to the artistic community, which was located down the street from my apartment and nestled between two universities and the St. Louis Symphony.

Frank had never been to the CWE, so I took him on a walking tour of the area after we ate. We shared an umbrella as we strolled through the rain under the enchanting streetlights. I showed him the local landmarks, and the blocks of historic houses, some with Mansard roofs and others with Corinthian columns and expansive porticos. The CWE offered a chemistry and excitement in each step. Even though Frank was from the suburbs, he showed a genuine interest in this neighborhood.

When he arrived at work the next day, Frank returned Rich's ten dollars and told him I was worth the money and time.

Frank was undeniably handsome with immense shoulders, rich black hair and beard, and soulful brown eyes. In addition, I got a taste of his perfect comedic timing and sharp intellect. I wasn't drawn to Frank that night because I was thinking about schoolwork. Also, he laughed like my younger brother and at 32, Frank was the same age as my brother, which made me somewhat uneasy. I was three years older and didn't consider a younger man to be dating material.

Frank grew on me, and for the first couple of months, we were friends and only friends. We played racquetball, walked, jogged, and went to the movies. I met his daughters, ages ten, five, and three, who accepted me immediately, and we included them in many of our activities. Our relationship deepened and we always enjoyed one another's company. As a couple, we fit together naturally and perfectly.

We fell in love.

As we grew closer, I came to realize Frank's engaging persona disguised a reluctance to express his feelings. He struggled with the words, "I love you." I teased him and said "*I one red rose you*," as a way to express my love without using the charged word Frank avoided. The phrase "*I one red rose you*" became part of our private language and endured long after Frank could verbalize his love for me.

Though we fell in love, we delayed marriage because I was on a need-based scholarship at my undergraduate institution, and his income would have skewed my financial aid. We moved, and I continued my education with the Yale University graduate school, where I received a fellowship from the National Institutes of Health. The fellowship covered my tuition and provided me with a reasonable stipend. More importantly, the university's financial policy no longer restricted my life plans. So, in the fall of 1989, two years after we moved to New Haven, Connecticut, Frank turned to me and said, "Why don't we get married in Saint Louis when we go home for the holiday break?" I knew I wanted to spend the rest of my life married to my best friend.

We planned the wedding for January 6, 1990, without realizing it was Epiphany, the twelfth day of Christmas, which was a nice surprise for our non-traditional but enchanting ceremony. I wore a long-sleeved white velvet dress with a button hat. Frank looked like Luciano Pavarotti in his black tuxedo. My nieces and Frank's daughters were bridesmaids; my oldest sister and brother accompanied me, substituting for my father. Several of our close friends and family members spoke about us individually and as a couple. The first friend cried during her contribution, and the tears continued to flow. When the scheduled family and friends finished, the pastor opened the invitation for other attendees to speak. Frank's oldest daughter, Angie, then age 15, delivered a tearful and moving speech about me and my relationship with her father. She was thrilled we met each other and was delighted I would become her stepmom. She praised her father as well from a place of profound gratitude. The congregation was in tears after she spoke. Our pastor said he had never participated in a wedding so full of joyous tears.

Everyone in attendance seemed touched by the experience in a profound way. In the receiving line after the ceremony, my brother-in-law, Tippy, hugged me earnestly and sobbed into my dress. His reaction was unusual, but he was expressing the heartfelt and soulful dynamics that we shared during the wedding service.

I was surprised and pleased at the unfolding of the events and touched deeply by the recognition from everyone. I cried inside with gratitude and was exhilarated by the outpouring of love and felt uplifted and valued. I wanted these feelings to last forever, just as I had anticipated my marriage would.

The reception was at an Elk's Lodge, and we hired a disc jockey for the music. The food was traditional Saint Louis fare; after all, no local wedding reception is complete without roast beef and mostaccioli. About 100 family members and friends attended.

Frank and I engaged in the traditional dance for the bride and groom. We selected Louis Armstrong's "What a Wonderful World" to acknowledge the wonder of our relationship. When we held one another on the dance floor, we smiled and expressed love to each other through our eyes, facial expressions, and close body language. About mid-way through the song, he looked at my face lovingly and said, "You are beautiful." His comment was special to me because he was a man of few words and even fewer compliments.

Frank's Arms: Introduction

By the end of the evening, his children were asleep on the floor on this warm, fun-filled, and loving evening.

Seven years later, Frank was diagnosed with systemic scleroderma.

Frank's Illness

Scleroderma loosely means "hardening of the skin." For some people, the disease is limited to the skin. For others, like Frank, it is systemic, and the internal organs harden.

His lungs were the first organ to be affected. Early in 1997, he went into the hospital for a lung biopsy to discover that the bottom third of his lungs had crystallized. The physicians at the hospital diagnosed Frank with lupus without treating him. I have no memory as to why the physicians did not offer medical intervention. Frank typically resisted such measures, so this may have played a factor in the decision. Nonetheless, we later learned that autoimmune disorders tend to mimic one another and often are misdiagnosed. Lupus was a misdiagnosis.

Frank mistrusted those in the medical profession. As a child, he had surgery on a testicle without being informed beforehand. He had no understanding of what was happening when he awoke in the hospital in pain with a "string" coming out of his penis. He also experienced the discomfort from a surprise tonsillectomy. As a result, he believed hospitals and physicians inflicted pain and didn't cure people of disease without causing other problems.

Accordingly, Frank was skeptical about the lupus diagnosis and didn't believe Western medicine would be able to help him find relief or offer a cure. Over the next year, he sought alternative forms of medicine to feel better. He saw a holistic chiropractor and tried treatments with herbs and energy work, but the disease and symptoms worsened. He was not aligned with any primary care provider, so we went to my internist, who took one look at Frank and said, "You have scleroderma and need to see a rheumatologist." By this time, the skin on his forearms and just above his elbows was tight and looked as if he had invisible bands on his arms. Still, the flesh on the top of his arms was not restricted and looked like typical skin. Since we were not experienced in the medical profession, we did not make a connection between the tightening of his skin and his physical condition. The chiropractor and energy workers did not either, perhaps because scleroderma is a rare disorder, especially in males.

I wanted Frank to go to a top rheumatologist in our area. My internist advised us against it, indicating that it could take a long time to get an appointment and we would probably not see that rheumatologist anyway; patients frequently see a colleague rather than the lead or head physician. We took his advice and sought out a specialist in his office. That rheumatologist ordered blood tests, x-rays, biopsies, MRIs, CT scans, and more to determine the extent of the internal organ involvement. Despite extensive testing and interventions, we still didn't understand the scleroderma diagnosis.

Moreover, drawing blood on Frank's hardened skin proved difficult. Every time he went for a blood draw, we were concerned the technician would be unable to do it. Frank would always ask, "Are you a good sticker?" The only person on whom we could rely for this was the phlebotomist in the rheumatologist's office; she was familiar with Frank's case and a seasoned technician. Frank needed sophisticated, experienced practitioners consistently because his case was so complicated. We could relax when he went to his rheumatologist's office if the phlebotomist was available.

Frank's heart was the next organ attacked. He avoided traditional medical intervention, even after connecting with the rheumatologist, until he had congestive heart failure in September 1998. He felt so sick that he did not go to work for four days, which was highly unusual for Frank. Early one morning, still resisting treatment, he told me that when he tried to lie down, he felt like he was being smothered. I convinced Frank he needed help.

Before this event, I had taken a supportive role as Frank explored ways to feel better, and I felt comfortable with the unconventional treatments he chose. But with this obvious emergency and decline in his physical condition, I shifted into a protective mode. I was alarmed and concerned about his condition but suppressed my emotions. I recognized we had to get Frank medical intervention as quickly as possible and did not have the luxury to cry or lose control. Also, I intuitively knew to model strength and determination so he would have confidence in his situation and in me as his caregiver and advocate.

I immediately called the rheumatologist at about 6:00 a.m. and described his symptoms to her. "Put him on the phone," she said. "I'll be able to tell by listening to him what's going on." She talked to Frank and then asked to speak to me.

"Take him to the hospital right now," she said.

Frank was reluctant and afraid to go to the hospital, but I convinced him. If I had done nothing, he would have died that evening. Frank was admitted to the hospital and then his arrhythmia became apparent after we arrived. All night, his condition was "touch and go." The rheumatologist consulted a cardiological electrophysiologist, and she installed a pacemaker-defibrillator unit into the left side of his chest because his heart was compromised. He would need the pacing from the unit if his heart rate dropped too low and the defibrillator if it beat too quickly. There was no going back. Frank was seriously ill.

I anxiously waited for several hours in fear and uncertainty while he was in surgery for the placement of the unit. I meditated and talked to a family member, which was a nice form of social support for me. Although I became accustomed to sitting and waiting for long intervals during his treatments, patience and "letting go" were not my strengths. I recognized I had no control over the outcome and "stayed put" as his wife and advocate. Reinhold Niebuhr's Serenity Prayer (1944) came in handy for me and helped allay some of my fear: "God grant me the serenity to accept the things I cannot change; the courage to change the things I can; and the wisdom to know the difference."

When the cardiologist finished, she told me this was one of her top two most difficult installations. Because of his past resistance to medical intervention and the condition of his heart, she asked me to promise her that Frank would never go off his heart medications. I promised.

Frank was on 10 to 12 medicines, some of which had harsh side effects that often made him feel worse; he hoped they were helping him. As a result, he was meticulous about tracking his dosages and keeping records. I monitored his regimen and created a grid to determine which combination of the drugs had a synergistic or potentiating effect. Together, we kept my promise that he would take his medications, particularly those for his heart.

Overall, Frank's skepticism about the outcome from treatment was on target. At this point, the medical interventions could only address his symptoms. Frank's disease had advanced too far for stem cell or bone marrow treatment. Though he had to rely on pharmaceuticals and intermittent tests that monitored the progression of his disease, his mindset and body were ready for every battle.

Over the years and with each new setback, his body regrouped and his mind fought and refused defeat. Even with a diagnosis of an incurable autoimmune disorder, Frank was always optimistic about life and his prognosis. He laughed and purposefully made jokes that made other people comfortable in the medical setting. It was easy for Frank to minimize his disease until it took its final toll. He could have passed as a healthy person to someone who didn't know him, up until his last six months.

Illness and intervention simply became our way of life.

My Gift to Frank

I SAVED ENOUGH FREQUENT FLYER MILES for two first-class, round-trip tickets to Europe. Frank and I flew to Paris and took a train to a small town in Austria near the German border.

The trip was my gift to him a few years after his physical troubles began.

We believed he had only one living relative in Austria on his paternal grandmother's side, a sister, and none related to his grandfather. I encouraged Frank to meet her and to see the place where his grandparents were raised, to get in touch with his roots. Frank's paternal grandparents came from the same town but did not know one another until they settled in St. Louis to start a new life. They married and had two children, one of which was Frank's father.

Frank's grandfather died when he was nine, and Frank was devastated by his death. His father passed away when Frank was in his early thirties, shortly after I met him. His grandmother, Anna, was a loving soul and a great storyteller. She talked to us many times about her childhood experiences in Austria. We spent hours, sometimes all day, in her company, sharing lunch and dinner because we couldn't pull ourselves away. I developed a fondness for her and understood why Frank was drawn to her. Anna reminded me of my deceased mother: generous, kind, warm. I was inconsolable when Anna died from a heart attack, as I relived the loss of my mother. And I was still missing Anna fifteen years later when we went to Europe.

Our first surprise in Austria came when Frank's cousin, August, a relative from his grandmother's side, met us at the train station and drove us to our hotel. As we rounded the first corner, we spotted a fleet of parked Mercedes trucks with SCHERTLER, Frank's last name, displayed on the marquis and side of the trucks. Our mouths dropped open. We learned a whole wing of the town had relatives from his grandfather's family.

This was a blessing for Frank to discover he had many relatives in Austria and for them to learn about us. The townsfolk heard about us coming, and they gave us the "red carpet" treatment, with a reception in our honor at the town hall, presents, lunches and dinners. The mayor took us to dinner, and the town's archivist tapped us for information on the family's lineage in St. Louis. In the process we learned Frank had a family crest on his grandfather's side in Austria.

We met his grandmother's sister, Lydia, who was a loving and giving person. We shared meals with her and enjoyed her stories, with our German-English dictionaries in tow.

One of his cousins, Burkhard, owns a shoe store. When I visited his store, he gave me a solid piece of advice: "Never go shopping when you need something." I still embrace that recommendation because shopping out of necessity causes us to spend more and not choose wisely.

I was touched by the town's people's friendliness. The hotel manager offered us his car for use and did not ask us

Frank's Arms: My Gift to Frank

for a credit card for the room until we brought the topic up on departure.

The trip had an indescribable impact on Frank, me, and those in Austria; the connection generated an abundance of family members and a legacy and anchor for his extended family at home, including his children. Frank was gratified and enriched by the trip. Most likely, it played a part in the delay of his serious physical deterioration.

This long overdue reunion was a universal gift inspired by divine intervention. Frank was the link and the instrument for the joy and celebration. I served by initiating the trip.

Taking Care of Myself

During one of Frank's hospital stays early in his illness, I saw the fear and confusion on his face when I was about to leave the hospital for the evening. I couldn't bear to abandon him so I stayed with him for 48 hours and slept in his room. My own resistance was down because of restless sleep and the stress of caring for Frank, so I got the flu and a high fever. I needed four days to recover. During that time, I couldn't visit him or respond to his needs. My brief illness made me realize that if I didn't take care of myself, I couldn't take care of Frank. We would be like two sinking ships.

Over time, I learned that even when I didn't know whether he was going to make it through the night, I needed to go home and get a good night's sleep. For me, this was a must. On a typical day, I had no way of knowing whether my visit would go smoothly or if any complications would occur. I had to be physically strong and mentally ready for whatever we were to face, making critical decisions in the moment.

As I reflect back, I realize I did many things to take care of myself. Like most people, my life was full even without Frank's illness. I was able to juggle my job and be Frank's primary caregiver, but to be strong for Frank, I participated in activities that healed my soul and strengthened me energetically.

Deborah L. Phelps, Ph.D.

At about the time Frank was diagnosed with scleroderma, I was participating in 90-minute integrated breath sessions every Tuesday afternoon with Tom Tessereau, a healer and breath worker. We engaged in breathing patterns to help remove toxins and calm the body and mind. I felt relaxed, peaceful, lighter, and centered after each session. Because of the benefits I received, I cleared my schedule so I could breathe during lunch every possible Tuesday.

As Frank's condition progressed, I intuitively recognized my need for support and took advantage of as many opportunities as possible to attend healing events, especially when there were lulls in Frank's treatment. One of the more profound experiences I had was at a rejuvenation retreat in Northern California, where a healer from Australia, Kerry Henwood, worked on me, using Tibetan Pulsing and Craniosacral Therapy. During this session, my heart chakra/center opened with a "poof" and that activation lasted for hours. I was amazed and reassured by that encounter and felt loved, peaceful, and stronger. It awakened an awareness in me that continues in my heart center as I respond to sadness, joy, or love in nature, humanity, and in the arts. Generally, I had resisted feeling anything during energy and bodywork sessions, so when this pronounced reaction occurred, I believed this treatment worked for me, at least on an energetic level.

When I returned home, I investigated both modalities and learned that the Upledger Institute teaches craniosacral therapy regularly in a variety of cities and practitioners use a light touch to release restrictions in the craniosacral system (cranium and sacrum) to promote healing and balance. After a lengthy search, I found only a description of Tibetan pulsing in a book on Tibetan healing. The procedure moves the client from mind to heart in an inner transformation process. However, I found no practitioners.

During a workshop in California, I got in touch with nature. The school emphasized the importance of cardinal directions from Native American and Freudian perspectives, and we were given assignments to address issues related to the north, south, east, and west in groups but independently from the other students. The east was related to spirituality, the south to the inner child, the north to the parent within us, and the west to our emotions. One of our assignments was to walk west on a road in the desert at night to get in touch with our feelings. The Milky Way blazed with no lights from the town to interfere. For protection, we carried a rattle to ward off rattlesnakes, and we took off in separate directions. The assignment worked, because on that beautiful starry night in the desert, I cried as I walked along the road and thought about my father's lack of acceptance. I realized that my perspective was probably inaccurate and that self-acceptance was the message I was to receive. I asked myself, "How can you be accepting and present for Frank if you do not accept yourself? How can you teach your students to accept others, if you do not model self-acceptance?" I felt lighter and liberated. All of the experiences with nature at this school fortified my soul and my role as Frank's caregiver.

I made several trips to Sedona, Arizona, to re-energize in its special metaphysical atmosphere and reconnect with nature in a way I couldn't do in St. Louis. During the early stages of his illness, Frank accompanied me. We hiked through red rock canyons and the energetically charged vortexes and often relaxed in the dry desert air. The vortexes in Sedona emit spiritual energy that can be complementary to prayer, meditation and healing. Many people/pilgrims connect to the energy for guidance, inspiration, and clarity. I often opened up to the vortex energy for guidance. We visited sacred Native American sites and participated in pipe ceremonies. We had multiple appointments for different bodywork modalities, some of which were profoundly healing. On one trip, I attended a sweat lodge ceremony, which cleansed and invigorated me.

The other refreshing and inspirational part of my Sedona visits was stopping by my maternal aunt's house in Phoenix and staying a day or two. We had long talks with her on her patio and enjoyed the temperate weather, gentle breezes, and the sunsets. My Aunt Betty was a loving, gracious, and independent woman, who was full of wit. My mother passed away in 1979 and Aunt Betty, like Frank's grandmother, represented the maternal presence I missed and cherished. My visits with Betty (and my other aunts) gave me a connection to my mother and comforted me. I could see my mother in each of them and they reinforced that with kind, mother-like compliments. Late one afternoon, Aunt Betty turned to me and said, "Your mother would be so proud of you." She gave me reassurance to continue with my academic and bodywork endeavors. I felt her love.

Many of the trips to California and Sedona were invitations from my network of friends who practiced and participated in energy and bodywork. We were all eager to learn and grow spiritually, emotionally, physically, and mentally. I do not know what I would have done without their support; they were a lifeline for me during Frank's illness.

Frank's Arms: Taking Care of Myself

Closer to home, I engaged in energy and bodywork and took classes in my quest for self-care. I had a standing bi-weekly Craniosacral Therapy appointment with Sue Costa that comforted me and soothed my physical aches and pains. It also gave me clarity and insight into questions I had about interpersonal relations and spiritual issues. I participated in many guided meditations with Choa Kok Sui, Billy Topa Tate, and Sri Sri Ravi Shankar in person and on CDs. I took classes to become a Reiki master in Usui Reiki and finished the second level in Karuna Reiki. When applied to healing, Usui Reiki addresses the body, mind and spirit and accelerates our ability to heal by redirecting the energy all around us into the client. Karuna Reiki refers to Reiki of compassion. Both forms take you down a permanent centered, loving path from which you cannot and do not wish to return. I became a massage therapist and took classes in healing touch and Pranic healing; in addition, I moved up to level three in Craniosacral Therapy. Each of these techniques helped ground and guide me and enhance my energy and bodywork skills. But time was the enemy, and as Frank's health worsened, I couldn't fit in everything. We had too many emergencies, and I stopped my educational pursuit of Craniosacral Therapy, although I continued to receive healing. Because I learned how to practice healing on others, I was able to work on Frank.

I engaged in Reiki circles with friends and acquaintances at local massage schools and spiritual centers. I participated in what we called "angel repair" workshops with my friends because we referred to ourselves as healing angels. During these sessions, we used healing modalities to work on one another. The sessions with my gifted friends were full of grace and peacefulness and had much value in terms of insight and encouragement to move toward equilibrium. I received and gave many blessings during the sessions with beautiful, soulful friends.

I attended holistic fairs and went to a psychic once at a fair out of curiosity because I had never been to one. However, none of her predictions came true. I volunteered for one year as the vice president on the board of directors for the Living Insights Center, a local spiritual and religious center that is inclusive of all spiritual and religious perspectives. My role as vice president expanded my religious knowledge and spiritual base; but I was distracted with the seriousness of Frank's condition, and most of the time, my mind was more on Frank than the board meetings.

Even with all the self-care techniques in which I engaged, I intermittently felt overtaxed. In the later stages of Frank's illness, I came close to my limit in terms of advocacy. Pushing for results became increasingly difficult as Frank's condition deteriorated and it began to wear on me mentally, emotionally, and physically. It seemed my oversight of Frank's care could never end for fear his health would be jeopardized. For example, I planned to attend a concert one evening. On the way there, I learned that the staff at Frank's rehab center hadn't changed his diaper for an extended period of time, despite the fact that he had diaper rash. They also had delayed giving him a bath for hours when he was anticipating this soothing care. On my only night off in weeks, I took time to make repeated phone calls to the center, addressing ascending levels of the staff to get some response to Frank's needs.

I became weary, almost like I had no tools left in my toolbox.

Frank's Arms: Taking Care of Myself

I had hoped the demands of Frank's care would lessen. I was so tired after so many years in the advocacy role that I was losing the necessary heart for the constant decision making and problem solving. I began to dread making demands on the health care workers, though I knew I must. Frank's reactions to his illness and my desire to meet his every need created internal conflict for me.

If I had used Deepak Chopra's strategies, I might have alleviated some of the distress of being a caregiver. The Law of Least Effort is one of the recommendations in Chopra's *The Seven Spiritual Laws of Success*. He advises us to get out of our own way, do nothing, and go with the flow. I could have worked toward advocating with less emotional distress. Chopra also recommends we count our blessings and maintain an attitude of gratitude. I continue to work on this.

One night, I left Frank's rehab center late. When I woke the following morning, I felt as if someone had sucked the energy out of my body. I was zapped. I had reached a point of physical and emotional exhaustion. That fatigue level stayed with me for weeks and, ultimately, months. Re-energizing was a long, slow process.

All the healing work, classes, and trips gave me encouragement and enrichment. Most of these activities took place in the first five years of Frank's illness. They fed me energetically and spiritually and strengthened me for the difficult last two years of Frank's life. Because I took care of myself, I was able to be a stronger advocate for Frank.

Not everyone will find support and self-care in the ways I did. Nonetheless, self-care is a form of advocacy with positive impacts on one's emotional, physical, and spiritual health. Whatever form the caregiver or widow chooses will serve that purpose.

PART TWO

MEDICAL INTERVENTIONS

Three Months to Live

IN 1998 MY WORLD CHANGED.

A nurse called me from Frank's beside in the cardiac intensive care unit (CIC) to answer a call from his rheumatologist. The doctor didn't waste any time delivering her message.

"Debbie, I'm so glad to reach you." With barely a breath between sentences, she launched the news: "Frank doesn't know how seriously ill he is."

I don't remember saying anything. I only remember the rest of the rheumatologist's words. "He's dying. He has three months to live."

As I stood outside Frank's hospital room with a clear view of his room and bed, the rheumatologist's message put me in an altered state of existence. After I hung up, I robotically walked into his room and acted as if nothing had happened. I didn't tell Frank the news of the prognosis. Neither did his rheumatologist.

Frank died of complications from scleroderma nearly seven years after that phone call. During those years, we rode an emotional, physical, and spiritual roller coaster ride with a number of near misses and countless trips to the emergency room (ER) and hospital.

This single phone call in the CIC after the installation of his pacemaker-defibrillator unit set the stage for difficult dynamics and two different realities for Frank and me. Because of her prediction, each time we went to the ER, I was concerned that he might be dying. Since the rheumatologist did not tell Frank her prognosis, he perceived each medical emergency as a temporary obstacle to overcome. From September 1998 until Frank's death in June 2005, my perspective on his physical condition differed from his, which complicated my job as his caregiver and advocate.

I'm unsure what kind of effect withholding this information had on Frank's outcome. I'm hoping it slowed the progression of his disease. The inside knowledge on his prognosis distressed and concerned me. Whenever I brought up the severity of his illness, Frank told me I was being negative, which is partially why I chose not to share the three-month prognosis with him.

Frank's rheumatologist shared it with me alone, on the phone away from Frank. Perhaps she wanted to protect him or give him hope while making his condition clear to me as his caregiver and advocate. Part of her concern about his state of mind was that he laughed and frequently made jokes in the hospital. That was his nature, but she misunderstood his behavior because she did not have a history with him. He didn't fit the mold of a patient with the severity of his condition. Nevertheless, his perpetual optimism and humor were useful in uplifting himself and those of us around him in the uncertain and unchartered waters we were navigating.

LESSONS AND REFLECTIONS

From this event, I learned that prognosis is difficult at best and that physicians act from training and experience to predict outcomes. Medical treatment is sometimes referred to as an art rather than a science. The timeline on the prognosis was wrong, but was I right not to share it with Frank? I believe being honest and sincere is a good idea; and as such, I had an internal conflict about withholding information.

As Frank's illness progressed, his rheumatologist consistently hesitated to give me a prognosis when I asked for one. I'm guessing her resistance was based on his having outlived her prediction for so long. After a number of inquiries, I pressed her and said, "If it was your husband or son, you would want to know." Then she gave me a straightforward response to my question with more specifics on his condition.

As time passed, I knew my perspective on Frank's physical situation was skewed by the early "misprognosis." I'm unsure assigning right or wrong to my decision to withhold the information from Frank has any benefit. As caregivers, we can only do the best we can with the information we have, while evaluating the situation and thinking clearly as an advocate. Admittedly, this task is difficult.

My perspective from seven years of his illness is that the patient and the caregiver have separate but complementary roles and can team up to possibly change or postpone the outcome. Frank's attitude, courage, and strength prolonged his life. My steadfast and heartfelt advocacy gave breath to his determination to fight his illness.

Gallbladder Surgery

IN THE SPRING OF 2002, FRANK WENT TO the hospital for what we thought was going to be gallbladder surgery, an invasive yet routine procedure. For us, the procedure became anything but routine.

The surgeons explored Frank's abdomen with a laparoscope but stopped because Frank had a significant amount of scar tissue in his abdomen. As a result, they made an abdominal incision to remove his gallbladder. They discovered the scar tissue from his scleroderma was so severe that the bile ducts had solidified and had ceased functioning, requiring them to reconstruct new bile ducts from a portion of his intestines. Instead of a one-hour laparoscopic procedure, Frank had to endure major abdominal surgery lasting several hours and creating additional complications.

During the surgery, they gave Frank general anesthesia and inserted a breathing tube (intubation) to ensure he received oxygen during the procedure, a typical course of action with surgery. Normally, after surgery is complete and the patient is stable, they remove the breathing tube once the patient can breathe independently. In Frank's case, when they removed the tube, he went into cardiac arrest (his defibrillator-pacemaker unit was off during the surgery). Given his history of heart complications, his medical team surmised that removing the breathing tube caused the arrest. Because his heart wasn't beating and he wasn't breathing on his own, they reinserted the breathing tube.

The anesthesiologist responded to his condition by using paddles to shock his heart back into rhythm. In her attempts to revive him, she repeatedly shocked him with the paddles even when his heart was back in rhythm and he was fully awake.

Once the medical team decided his heartbeat had stabilized, they moved him into the intensive care unit (ICU).

When I arrived in his ICU room, I was stunned to see Frank's condition. He had tape on his face and tubes in his nose and throat, and he was unable to move his body or extremities because of the anesthesia. As the effects of the anesthesia began to wear off, he was able to move only his eyes and when he rolled them in an attempt to communicate with me, I could tell he wanted my attention. Something was wrong. After he was able to move his arms, he pointed to his face and turned his head in a "no" gesture.

He wanted the breathing tube taken out.

"Frank, if you keep moving your hands, I'm gonna strap them down," the ICU nurse said when she noticed Frank moving his hands and pointing to his face.

"Over my dead body," replied Frank's daughter, Mandy. Thank goodness she was there.

Frank clearly hated the tube, so I asked questions, some of many I would ask throughout our times in hospitals. I learned they planned to keep the breathing tube in his

Frank's Arms: Gallbladder Surgery

throat until the next day without sedating him. I knew I had to help him.

I left the ICU to focus on what I needed to do. I didn't come to a conscious solution immediately; but when I returned, I knew I had to talk the medical team into either sedating Frank or removing the breathing tube. Frank was desperate and counting on me. In response, I moved fully into my role as Frank's advocate with a strong determination to get results for him.

I asked Frank's nurse to "either put him out or take it out." She refused, so I approached the resident and then the attending physician and made the same request. Calling upon my background in research, I reasoned with them: "Removing the breathing tube may not be related to his heart stopping. You only know the two conditions happened at about the same time," I told them. "You don't know that they are related. If he wants it out and he is uncomfortable, won't you give him the benefit of the doubt and remove it? If his heart stops again, you can always stick it back in."

I persuaded the attending physician, who agreed to remove the breathing tube (extubate) if Frank's breathing and heart remained stable for 20 minutes longer. By this time, the breathing tube had been in for several hours. When there is an object down your throat and you are awake, even 10 seconds is too long.

Frank had to wait.

Much of surviving in hospitals involves waiting. Mandy and I stayed at Frank's side to ride out the next 20 minutes with him. He was anxious and we comforted him with soothing and encouraging words. I was constantly eyeing the clock. When 15 minutes had passed, I began to press the nurse for action, "Okay, you agreed to take it out in 20 minutes; there are 5 minutes left." I repeated my message every minute until it was out.

As soon as the nurse removed the tube, Frank said, "Thank you, I felt like I was being smothered to death." We learned the breathing tube had been in his throat at an odd angle, making the experience even worse for Frank than we imagined. After they withdrew the tube, we watched Frank closely, looking for signs of cardiac distress, but none appeared. We finally relaxed, at least for this round of events.

I later learned the breathing tube was not related to Frank's cardiac arrest after the surgery. Sometimes anesthesiologists can misjudge and give a patient too much anesthesia, which was true in Frank's treatment and likely triggered his cardiac arrest.

LESSONS AND REFLECTIONS

This event empowered me as Frank's advocate. I asked the medical staff probing questions when I needed clarification, wanted an explanation in layman's terms, or needed to challenge the care being provided if I did not agree with the treatment, even in the ICU.

When the ICU nurse could not respond to Frank's need to remove the tube, I asked the resident, who had more rank and power. But his response, like the nurse's, told me he wouldn't or couldn't act. So I approached the attending physician, who had the power to help Frank. I persuaded the physician to honor Frank's request.

Throughout this episode, I had to rely on my intuition to resolve this issue because I was working from the disadvantage of not having medical training. I was the outsider fighting the system, but I had the advantage of being the insider in terms of assisting an ailing and distressed loved one. And I experienced firsthand the power differential that exists between the medical professionals (doctors and nurses) and the laypersons (the patients, caregivers, and advocates). In this case, Frank was powerless because he could not speak for himself, and he was depending on me to get the results that he needed. And that's what I did. I accepted the responsibility and went to battle for Frank.

The conviction to probe for more information came from my sociology background, which encouraged me to question everything. I knew that the more I understood, the better off we were in terms of Frank's treatment. The more I asked questions, the easier the process of helping Frank became. When Frank needed the breathing tube out, I did not take "no" for an answer. I pushed until they removed it. It helped that Frank went to a teaching hospital, a prime place for questioning. Teachers like to teach and I am a strong candidate for that kind of exchange.

In addition, my perspective and reaction to the breathing tube incident were partially based on sociological principles that "things are not what they seem" (Berger) and that we are to use our sociological imagination and be engaged in our social world (Mills)—to be active participants in our health care. These tenets gave me the confidence to question Frank's problematic medical experiences. Patients, caregivers, and advocates often feel uncomfortable questioning medical professionals and simply assume that the professionals say and do the absolute best for their patients all the time. But practitioners are human, not all-knowing or all-seeing beings. They don't always have all the answers and sometimes make educated guesses as a result. Communication between all parties can benefit decision making and the health care outcome, despite the fact that the typical caregiver and patient do not have medical training.

Infected Stitch

THE COMPLICATIONS FROM HIS GALLBLADder surgery continued when Frank left the hospital. In May 2002, as we were sitting at home, Frank called out to me from the living room, "Debbie! Debbie, there is something coming out of me." He walked down the hall toward me with his shirt raised. Green pus was coming out of a nickel-sized hole in his abdomen.

I ran next door to my neighbor, who was a nurse, and asked her to take a look at Frank's stomach. Frank and I were hoping that we could avoid the ER that evening and go instead to the doctor's office during normal business hours. My neighbor confirmed that we could probably wait. The pus oozed about the size of a tablespoon consistently throughout the night. I kept wiping it away and it kept oozing. And we waited through the night.

The back story on this is we avoided the ER as much as possible because of Frank's experiences there. We often rode out his episodes in the hope that the crises would pass. Since his skin and internal organs were compromised, his case was complicated. The treatment in the ER was sometimes torturous. As I mentioned, his skin was tough and hard to penetrate, and his veins were small and had a tendency to roll.

One time, shortly before his gallbladder surgery, Frank went to the ER with severe abdominal pain. The staff attempted to penetrate his skin for an IV eight times. Each time, as the needle poked into his thickened skin, he moaned in pain. Finally, a pediatrician, more skilled at placing IVs in small veins, was called in and placed the IV line into his neck. All the while, Frank had intense abdominal pain and kept asking for something for relief, but they would not give it to him. When I asked why and pleaded with the staff at the desk, someone responded, "We don't want to mask the symptoms, so we have to wait for the surgeons to take a look at him." In the meantime, he kept asking for relief, and I kept asking for some medication to relieve his pain. In addition to those traumas, twelve hours passed before they admitted him to a hospital room.

So, when his abdomen opened up following the gallbladder surgery, we did not rush back to the ER.

The following morning, I took him to the doctor's office. He was admitted directly to the hospital for treatment without having to go through the ER. His doctor was able to bypass it with an order for direct admission into the hospital. The source of the problem was an infected stitch from the gallbladder surgery. The treatment plan was to clean the wound twice a day and to pack it with gauze and let it heal from the inside out.

Frank had plans to ride in a pick-up truck to Texas for a business trip just a few days later. I was against his going. When he mentioned his plans to the doctor and me, we exchanged a glance that said, "Yeah, right." Most people would not have been strong enough to go and could not have withstood the bumpy ride in the truck. I was dealing with a tenacious man with strength and courage.

Frank's Arms: Infected Stitch

I thought, "If anybody can do this, Frank can." And he did. He learned how to clean and pack his own wound and left for Texas with his long strips of gauze, scissors, tweezers, and saline solution.

Normally the treatment would have been delegated to me; but in this case, Frank had to learn how to do it. Eventually he overcame this hurdle and his body healed from the infected stitch.

Deborah L. Phelps, Ph.D.

LESSONS AND REFLECTIONS

This incident reinforced the idea of the importance of self-determination to get well and one's active participation in health care. Frank was able to administer treatment to himself, which empowered him in the face of a difficult situation.

One of the messages from the medical sociology literature is to be an active rather than passive participant in one's health care. The most common term for this is "mutual participation." One assertion from this perspective is that an active participant is more likely to get better and stay better longer. If mutual participation occurs, the practitioner is more informed and the patient is on stronger ground. Fundamentally, one could ask this question: Who knows one's body and symptoms better than the patient? Frank and I were definitely active participants in his health care, at times maybe overly active.

Beginning of the End

THE GALLBLADDER SURGERY AND INFECTED stitch foreshadowed the medical events that followed. Two years later, in 2004, the beginning of the most difficult times in his illness started one Saturday morning at a local diner. Shortly after our food arrived, Frank leaned back in the booth and said he felt unwell. I took one bite of my breakfast sandwich and noticed that Frank was too weak to cut up his pancakes. He looked pale. I moved into full caregiver mode. As I rushed to the exit, I shouted to the server behind the counter, "My husband has a heart condition. I'm going for the car."

I drove our car onto the sidewalk close to the diner entrance. My mind was set on driving him to his primary hospital where they were familiar with his condition. When I rushed back into the diner, two servers were standing on each side of Frank, comforting him, and holding a cold towel on his neck. In the couple of minutes I was gone, he had worsened. I had to call 911, which is something we had avoided until then. I stood in the middle of the diner and hollered, "Cell phone? I need a cell phone. Can somebody give me a cell phone?"

I felt numb as I watched the ambulance arrive and the emergency medical technicians treat Frank. One of the technicians said to me, "We're taking him to 'X' Hospital," which was around the corner and up the hill. "Can't you take him to his primary hospital?" I asked. "All of his doctors are associated with that hospital." I turned to some of the folks in the restaurant and asked if anyone knew anything about "X" Hospital. No one made a comment. The EMTs, both males, insisted on taking him there, explaining that standard procedure was to take an unstable patient to the nearest emergency facility. I had to give in. I followed the ambulance to the hospital in our car.

When I entered Frank's ER room, he was sitting up bright-eyed and smiling and he delivered one of his usual lines to me: "We've got it surrounded!" From his perspective, this was just another bump in the road. But not from mine. A change had occurred, and I knew Frank's condition was worsening.

Shortly after I arrived, I began to call friends and relatives to inquire about the competence of the facility. Nobody could give me a comforting answer because they didn't know, so I pulled strings until I was successful in getting Frank transferred to his primary hospital, where the providers had immediate access to his treatment records. I called his rheumatologist and cardiologist and questioned the staff at both hospitals. I stopped bugging people only when I knew the transfer was set. After working for six hours to get the transfer, I was an emotional wreck, due in part to my assessment of his physical deterioration and the inside knowledge about his prognosis.

I hated to let go or lose control in providing his transportation for treatment. One time, when his pacemaker-defibrillator unit fired in the middle of the night, I pulled the car up into the yard and adjacent to our elm tree and deck, about as close as I could possibly get to him. I helped him dress and he leaned on me as we walked

Frank's Arms: Beginning of the End

to the car. He laid down in the backseat, and I played soft opera for him during the ride to the hospital to give him comfort. Up until that January morning in the diner, we had been able to get him to the doctor's office or hospital on our own.

This was the beginning of the end in my mind.

> ## Lessons and Reflections
>
> *This incident taught me that I needed to pay careful attention to Frank's symptoms and to seek help when needed. This incident also reinforced the fact that I had the power to make changes in Frank's treatment plan. I was able to have him transferred to his hospital and doctors by being persistent. Frank's sudden decline was a significant turning point for me. It reminded me the extent to which Frank was in denial about the progression of his disease; I understood that I encouraged that to some degree by humoring him and withholding the rheumatologist's 1998 prognosis.*

Feeding Tube Removal

TIME PASSED AFTER THE JANUARY 2004 diner incident and Frank's condition continued to worsen. Throughout the winter of 2004-2005, he coughed relentlessly. His rheumatologist prescribed antibiotics and cough syrup but to no avail. He kept coughing and was particularly bad at night. Finally, during one of his hospital stays in May 2005, the providers determined the cause of his cough. Frank had been aspirating food and drink into his lungs for months because two-thirds of his esophagus had shut down. He had become so weak during this time that he couldn't raise himself or walk. His medical team recommended the placement of a permanent feeding tube directly into his stomach that would bypass his need to swallow food or liquids and, thus, would greatly reduce his chances of aspiration and lung infections. The tube would also allow him to get much-needed nourishment. They had to delay the surgery because the only two surgeons at his primary hospital who were qualified to do the procedure were attending a conference together and would not return for four days. As an interim fix, they placed a temporary nasogastric feeding tube from his nose to his stomach because they were concerned about his weight loss, weakness, and muscle deterioration.

Frank hated the temporary tube. The moment I saw him after the procedure, he asked me to arrange to have the feeding tube removed, and he repeated, "I would rather die than have this tube in me." For Frank this was another tube in his throat, causing him distress. The memory of the breathing tube after his gallbladder surgery resurfaced and added to his anxiety. Frank knew how I battled for him to get the breathing tube taken out and he expected me to do the same to get the temporary feeding tube removed. His words may have been hyperbole. I don't think he would have rather died, but he knew his comment would make me take action quickly. At 2:00 p.m., shortly after the tube was placed, I began negotiating to get it removed.

I started by reaching out to the nursing staff. Once again, I had to go up the chain of command. I talked to a nursing supervisor, intern, resident, attending physician, and even the hospital chaplain in an attempt to fulfill Frank's request. Each time I made contact with the hospital staff, I received resistance to the idea. Each time that occurred, I asked to speak to the person's supervisor, sometimes inquiring, "Who is your boss? Give me the name and contact information for your boss."

Frank was stressed and agitated during the process, which was unusual and added pressure for me to get the job done. I was distressed but was able to keep my cool and stay focused until the mission was accomplished at about 9:00 p.m., seven hours later.

With the temporary tube out, we waited four more days until the surgeons returned and placed the permanent feeding tube into his stomach. Each day as Frank went without nutrition, he weakened. Unfortunately, even after the permanent tube was placed, Frank did not improve. Frank's intestines were malfunctioning and shutting down. He wasn't absorbing the nutrients the tube was delivering. Medical intervention could do little more for him. After consulting with his rheumatologist and the other members of his medical team, Frank agreed to transfer to a rehab center.

His treatment had reached a point of diminishing returns, and his medical team understood what rehab would do for him and what it meant in the long run: Frank would continue to decline regardless of the treatment setting.

Lessons and Reflections

The tube removal episode taught me that installing a temporary tube is easier than removing it. His medical team saw the insertion of a tube as a straightforward solution to a temporary problem. However, despite Frank's insistence that he be kept alive, he did not want the discomfort of the feeding tube. I chose to defend his desire to withdraw the tube.

This experience reinforced the idea that persistence can pay off in the role of advocacy. In this particular situation, I talked to at least half a dozen people on the hospital staff. I kept my approach assertive but non-threatening, and I kept asking until I was able to reach the goal of getting the tube removed.

I realize some caregivers soften their demands on medical and hospital personnel out of concern they will alienate the staff from themselves or their loved ones. I never experienced this concern, though, as I mentioned earlier, I did grow tired of having to demand Frank receive the care he needed. I'm glad I pushed on. I'm glad I advocated for Frank, even when I felt I couldn't go another step or make one more decision.

Do Not Resuscitate

Frank developed a living will (health care directive) in May 2002, and he appointed me as his durable power of attorney for health care. A living will provides guidelines for withholding or withdrawing treatment. It also addresses whether to prolong procedures in case of an emergency or progression of a disease. The document outlines the express wishes of the patient when he or she is unable to communicate. Up to that point, Frank had resisted talking about emergencies or death. His typical response to either topic was "That's negative," which frustrated and concerned me. Ultimately, Frank had a fear of dying and was unprepared to die or talk about anything related to his own death. In his mind, he had overcome each setback, and he figured that would continue. Nevertheless, he agreed to the living will under the guise that we would be developing one for each of us.

The procedures listed in our documents covered tube feeding, radiation, cardiopulmonary resuscitation (CPR), dialysis, and chemotherapy. I indicated in my version that I did not want chemotherapy, radiation, or dialysis by placing an "x" next to the appropriate line in the document. Frank left all of his lines blank, meaning that he wanted me, as his power of attorney and agent, to request just about everything possible to keep him alive. In some ways, his position contradicted the point of a living will to withhold or withdraw certain medical procedures in the event of an emergency. By leaving everything blank, I and his health care team understood that if he could no longer express his wishes, he wanted everything done to prevent his death. A Do Not Resuscitate (DNR) declaration was definitely not in Frank's plans.

Three years passed after we finalized his living will, and Frank continued to worsen. During Frank's next-to-last hospitalization, his rheumatologist had a serious talk with him early one morning about considering a DNR directive as part of his living will. She reminded him how miserable he was with the breathing tube after his gallbladder surgery and suggested he avoid having one installed when he was near death. She told us that CPR at that point in his illness would fail.

Frank was unhappy about having a DNR directive, but he agreed to go along with the rheumatologist's suggestions. He called me at home after his conversation with her and said in a sad voice, "We have something important to talk about."

I went to the hospital before work and he told me about their conversation. The rheumatologist made Frank understand little time remained. I knew Frank didn't want to hear this because he clung to the hope he would beat the disease. I worked my way through the wires and IV lines hooked up to him and climbed into his hospital bed. Lying side by side, hugging him gently from behind, I spoke softly and encouragingly to him. I'm unsure if my words gave him much comfort after learning that CPR would be ineffectual.

Frank wanted to live so badly, even through the worst of his scleroderma.

He had difficulty processing the decline in his condition and the change in his health care. My heart was breaking watching him face his coming death, but I was as attentive and present as possible while covering my own sadness.

That evening we discussed his medical situation and what measures he would like to be taken if he couldn't speak for himself. He completed a new living will. This time, he gave me the authority to direct a health care provider to withhold food and water should the need arise. He rejected using CPR and a ventilator, and he directed me to have his pacemaker-defibrillator unit turned off if necessary. His unit was programmed to fire five times if his heart went into fast rhythm, which can easily happen when the heart is struggling to survive. He understood that if the unit couldn't keep his heart balanced, CPR wasn't going to work either.

I witnessed the effects of the defibrillator on his body one night when we were asleep several years earlier. I reacted to the jolt and tried to determine what had happened on his side of the bed. Frank's description of the defibrillator firing was that it felt "like a horse kicking him." He had suffered a long time from the debilitating effects of scleroderma, and being kicked to death would be an unfair ending for Frank, not that any of this was "fair."

Nonetheless, a few weeks later while he was in the rehab center, Frank changed his mind. He didn't want a DNR order and he wanted to revise his living will for the second time. He wanted everything medically possible to be done to keep him alive: CPR, a ventilator, and the activation of his pacemaker-defibrillator unit. The rehab center staff reluctantly complied and changed the orders in his chart.

Frank's decision to reverse the living will again concerned me. I wanted to protect him from more suffering and knew life-prolonging interventions would fail. Legally, as long as Frank was able to express his own wishes, he controlled his medical care and the staff responded accordingly. This was true even though they knew he was incoherent at times as his disease progressed. Eventually, his facial expressions indicated he was not getting good blood flow to his brain and he became particularly anxious. He frequently hit the television remote and repeated, "I want English. I want English." He also moved the bed up and down with the remote. Frank typically did not perform small tasks with great anxiety and tension, so this concerned me. I kept my emotions bottled up and did my best to respond to his requests. I felt drained from the process but intended to support him, whatever it took.

A couple of days before Frank died, I met with his cardiologist, a resident, and his attending physician in the ICU. As his durable power of attorney, I was able to introduce a compromised approach to the use of his pacemaker-defibrillator for their consideration. The medical staff and I agreed to keep Frank's unit turned on, but with the stipulation that if his heart went into fibrillation and his unit fired once, we would hit the unit with a magnet to deactivate it and prevent Frank from getting shocked four more times when his heart was failing. We planned to keep the pacemaker component of the unit operational, because it functioned to maintain a steady rhythm without an obvious physical sensation for Frank. With the new arrangement for his defibrillator component, we protected Frank from pointless suffering while honoring his request to keep the unit active until the end of his life.

Lessons and Reflections

I learned a living will is a guideline and not a rule. When Frank was able to speak for himself about the direction of his medical care, his living will did not come into play. He had the power to add or subtract medical procedures, which complicated my position. I had to establish a compromise between Frank's desire to spare no medical intervention and my desire to spare him needless suffering.

I learned health care providers will attend to the patient according to the most recent living will and can accommodate verbal and written changes to the living will, regardless of how frequently the patient may make these changes. I also learned that doctors will work with advocates or family members. They will listen to them and honor their requests to the extent possible, provided there is no harm to the patient and the patient's legal documents are executed.

Finally, I learned that my husband, Frank, was one of the strongest and most courageous people I have ever known. He faced his fear and dealt with his impending death on his terms. He didn't let others persuade him from determining how or when he was going to die.

Comfort

ANYONE WHO HAS EMBRACED CAREGIVING and advocacy understands it's impossible to whitewash or slap a shiny veneer on the emotional pain of caring for someone who is terminally ill.

And yet, most who travel this journey would choose to do it again. We do it out of love. We do it out of a sense of duty. In my case, I also did it for another reason: whether we were in our cozy living room or in a sterile hospital room, there was no one's company I enjoyed more than Frank's. For that, I will be forever grateful.

When I visited him in the health care facilities, I often brought reading material and papers to grade, as I might have done during an ordinary evening or weekend at home. We talked, laughed, and shared stories, often with visitors. Frank had a magnificent sense of humor: our world was filled with laughter that often turned to tears. Being in each other's presence was delightful even in the worst of conditions.

Shortly before he died, Frank said he thought he was acting selfishly because I spent so much time and energy to support him. I reminded him we not only were husband and wife, we were friends and being with him as much as possible was easy. This, and Frank's complete and unconditional belief in me bound me to him. I treasured that faith.

We had days when we were not in emergency mode, and I was able to coast and be his caregiver on a less demanding level. In those instances, we went out to eat or to see a movie. Frank loved to go out to breakfast, and we did that as often as possible. When he ate, he cut everything on his plate before he took one bite. If he had eggs, bacon, and pancakes, he cut the bacon and eggs with a knife and fork and blended them together. Then, he buttered the pancakes and cut vertical and horizontal rows to make small chunks and poured syrup down each of the rows. Generally, I was finished with my breakfast by the time he had his food prepared. Frank was consistently methodical in his behaviors, in his personal life and in his professional life as an electrical engineer.

Sometimes we watched television together or music videos in the living room as Frank convalesced on the sofa. I sat at his feet and often cupped his toes and fingers between my hands using Reiki heat that emanated from my palms. Frank had developed Raynaud's disease with sores on his hands and feet and they were always cold. This comforting gesture enhanced our physical connection, especially during the last couple of years when our intimacy had diminished. Moreover, cradling Frank's toes and fingers was less physically and emotionally taxing than solving issues at the hospital or rehabilitation center.

Frank would often say to me, "You are such a comfort."

One evening when I returned from work I found Frank resting on the living room sofa. As I entered the room, he turned to me with a serious look on his face and said without preamble, "I love you dearly." I believe Frank's declaration came from his understanding of the

Frank's Arms: Comfort

seriousness of his illness coupled with his acceptance of the unconditional love I and others gave him.

There were times when Frank created a dynamic to keep me by his side. This was especially true in the last few weeks of his life when he would find ways to delay my departure from the rehab center.

For example, a few times when I was leaving for the night, he asked me to adjust his pillow. He would say, "No, adjust it again. Could you also…"

One incident that touched me deeply occurred when I brought the electric trimmer to shape his beard. After I finished the trim and was wrapping up the device, he pointed to a place on his face and said, "Over here, do it here." I unwrapped the trimmer, plugged it in, touched up his beard, and wrapped it again when he said, "Here! Do it here!" He repeated that request to keep me there. That incident was hard for me. I hung in for him as long as I could, giving him comfort in one of the few ways I could.

Unconditional support proved to be essential for Frank's well-being and for my peace of mind.

LESSONS AND REFLECTIONS

I learned through intuition and experience that treating a loved one with dignity and respect is paramount to emotional comfort, no matter what it takes to accomplish the task. Those suffering with terminal illness need to feel unconditional love and support from those closest to them, as the disease can gradually rob them of their dignity. Moreover, if the patient encounters health care providers who are neglectful or do not have good "bed-side manners," the loss of dignity and respect is more likely. Physical discomfort can be more easily tolerated if they believe they are not alone and that the care and advocacy come without hesitation or conditions.

I learned that comfort can take many forms, ranging from a smile or loving presence to a significant act of advocacy.

I learned that caregiving and advocacy are best without judgment.

I learned that dignity reflects back to the caregiver, creating a circular dynamic.

Death's Dress Rehearsal

EVEN THOUGH FRANK WAS NOT GETTING nutrition from the feeding tube, he was determined to regain strength in the rehab center. He mentioned in the hospital that he planned to gain one pound a week in the rehab center for a total of 20 pounds. Instead of gaining weight and strength in the center, he lost one pound a day for the first nine to 10 days. Then he did the unexpected: he gave up.

On a Wednesday afternoon, about 10 days before his death, he told me he wanted to die.

Since I was his advocate, he requested I summon all of the family and close friends to the rehab center, and he directed his physicians to disengage his feeding tube and pacemaker-defibrillator unit.

I call this episode "death's dress rehearsal."

A steady stream of people filed into his room that evening. They approached Frank and recognized him for his contributions to their lives. They came in groups of two or three, walked up to his bed, and spoke to him. They talked about his sense of humor and intelligence and told him how much they were going to miss him. Over the course of the evening about 20 to 30 people—his children, my siblings, our nieces, nephews, and other close relations—passed through his room at the rehab center.

Frank did not respond to anyone. He intentionally kept his eyes closed with his hands folded on his stomach in the posture of a corpse in a casket. Frank's children and I experienced what would be similar to his funeral. People were crying, yet none sobbed. This request to visit was so sudden that no one had time to prepare for it.

That evening I made arrangements with the cardiologist and rehab center staff to turn off the pacemaker-defibrillator unit and to disengage the feeding tube the following day. His cardiologist, so fond of Frank, cried when I telephoned her.

On Thursday, Frank's daughter, Peggy, and I waited all day for the cardiac technician to come. The tech began to cry shortly after she entered his room, which of course added to our sadness. She informed us that his heart was 97 percent dependent on the unit as she disconnected it at about 3:00 pm. He had a three percent chance of surviving the night.

The rehab staff members were reluctant to turn off the feeding tube. I think they viewed this request as something of an act of assisted suicide or passive euthanasia. Nevertheless, they complied on Thursday afternoon. His children and I waited all evening. We sat near his bed at the level of his body and watched his breathing, expecting he would exhale but not inhale. We worried about his readiness for death we thought was imminent.

Late in the evening, I left.

I was expecting bad news by morning, but I had to get some rest.

I woke up at dawn on Friday and called the rehab center for a report. Frank was sitting up in bed, alert, indicating to the staff that he wanted to retry coping with his condition and regaining his strength. I rushed to his side, and he asked me to contact the cardiologist and center staff to have his pacemaker-defibrillator unit and feeding tube reactivated. He explained he panicked and did not know how to respond to the news that he was losing weight so rapidly. To deal with the situation he shut himself off. When I telephoned his cardiologist and informed her about Frank's new mindset, she responded, "He can have the unit turned on and off as many times as necessary" and she gave me her cell phone number in case we needed to call her again. It didn't take long after my phone call to her for the same cardiac technician to make things operational. I realized turning a medical unit on is easier than turning it off.

Friday was a mixed blessing for me and his loved ones. We were relieved temporarily: Frank would be with us longer. However, as with all dress rehearsals, we knew the real event was yet to come.

Lessons and Reflections

This episode reminded me that we have no control over someone else's behavior. I went along with Frank's decision to give up – and then to fight again. I learned that patients facing death may be self-absorbed. Perhaps Frank's dress rehearsal was an example of this. However, I was reminded of Chopra's recommendation to do nothing, just allow.

It also reinforced the notion that practitioners care. Both Frank's cardiologist and the technician cried about turning off his cardiac unit. His cardiologist understood Frank's emotional and mental struggles and reflected this when she gave him permission to repeat his request for disengagement of his unit as many times as he wanted. That was generous and an emotional support to me.

Death

The following Monday, five days after death's dress rehearsal, I arranged for Frank to come home. This is what we both wanted. Frank had lived beyond anyone's prediction. I was given a crash course in how to care for him at home, including how to lift and move him. We were able to get everything arranged quickly, and Frank was to come into my care the following day.

The evening before he was to come home, Frank was in trouble again. He was exhibiting symptoms of congestive heart failure. We had to decide whether he should come home and ride it out or be transferred back to his primary hospital.

Frank opted for the hospital, which told me he continued to hope he could beat the disease. So, I put on my advocate cap and persuaded the nursing staff to set up the transfer, keeping in mind they had stopped medical intervention. I also had to convince them to transfer him to his primary hospital. I could request a specific hospital as long as Frank appeared to be stable. Frank and I planned for him to act as if he were not so seriously ill when the EMTs arrived. When they entered his room, I was delighted to see the drivers were female. I hoped they would relate to a female advocate and comply with my request. Frank did beautifully at faking his condition and it worked. They took him to our requested hospital. One of them was kind enough to call me when Frank was successfully placed in the ER.

Frank once said, "You don't know when you're going to go, but you know when you're not." Over the course of the seven years of his illness, Frank told me he wasn't ready to let go, that he had more to do, and he must have kept his conviction the last night in the rehab to choose the hospital again.

Frank received a visit from a pastor the rehab center recommended two days later at his request. We learned this pastor had healed people from terminal illness, implying Frank might receive a break. Frank, clinging to hope of some last-minute divine intervention, was eager to do anything to prolong his life. The pastor and Frank had a private discussion, and Frank didn't share the conversation with me. I let that go and didn't press him for the information in his weakened physical and mental condition. I believed the dialogue was sacred and between him and the clergyman.

One day later, when I was about to leave after a consultation with the cardiology team, Frank motioned for me to come close to him because he had something to tell me. By this time, he had difficulty breathing and could barely speak.

I leaned over him and put my ear close to his mouth. "They are going to revive me as many times as necessary. Only God decides when we are to go," he whispered.

Those were his last words. I entered the hall and waved good-bye, and he waved back.

He lost consciousness sometime during the night.

Frank's Arms: Death

Friday morning, the resident on his case called and requested I come to the hospital right away. His rheumatologist met me in Frank's room and summoned me into the hall. Speaking in a low voice and with Frank in my field of vision, she said, "Frank is not going to make it this time. He has 48 hours or less." One of the staff members recommended I invite our family members to come to pay him a last visit. His children joined me, and we sat with him all day with no response from him and no apparent change in his status.

At about 5:00 p.m. we decided to go to dinner since it looked as if he was in a holding pattern. While we were dining, Angie's cell phone rang. It was a member of the hospital staff telling her Frank had passed away. We were told that his heart stopped beating and he took his last breath. We rushed back to his side and when we arrived, his body was still warm. Ultimately, Frank's wish to be resuscitated was impossible. The defibrillator wasn't triggered because his heart did not go into the rapid beating that signaled the need for a shock. Frank was spared the sensation of any "horse kicks" and I have every reason to believe he passed away peacefully.

I kissed him and sat by his bedside with my hand on his arm, and I held it there until long after his body turned cold. His children and mom were the first to leave the ICU. My sister, niece and two of my close friends were with us, primarily to support me. One of my friends told me she saw his spirit in the room after he died and that he talked to her telepathically. He told her "I don't know what I was so scared about. This was easy." My friend had the sense that he stayed in spirit form the whole time we were there. I took her word for it because I did not detect his presence or hear anything from him.

The ICU staff members told us to take as much time as we needed, so a number of us, including my two dear friends, remained with Frank's body for several hours. My friends were the last to go. Before they left, I checked with the ICU staff again about the length of our visit to see if we overstayed our welcome. The staff member indicated that we could remain as long as we wanted. I intended to be the last one to leave so I could say a private good-bye to Frank.

When we were alone, I kissed him and said, "Good-bye, Frank. You're my friend." I walked away from his room for the last time with a heavy heart and deep sadness, barely putting one foot in front of the other one.

The events of the last day, including my walk from his room, were surreal. "Could this have happened? Was Frank dead? What did Frank's communication to my friend mean? Was this really the last time I would be his advocate in a medical setting? Will I really never be able to hold him again?" I went to sleep in our bed alone with these questions in mind.

Frank fought to the bitter end and never gave up hope he would win the battle with scleroderma. His rheumatologist said no scleroderma patient had ever lived beyond one year with a compromised heart. And yet, Frank lived seven years after this devastating complication. His rheumatologist suspected Frank hung on because he didn't want to leave me. I believed her.

Lessons and Reflections

By managing Frank's transfer to his primary hospital, I learned that persistence and determination prevail. We expected the best and set the stage for that to happen energetically and in our mindset. We were empowered by using teamwork and fortitude to meet our goal.

It was clear Frank had hope for his recovery. I knew I had to support Frank's wishes and I did, balancing the realities of his illness with his hope. I don't have regrets about how I cared for Frank. I found a way to protect him, to care for him, and to honor his request to revive him when we could. Frank was in charge, his arms were wrapped around his life with me by his side.

During the last week of Frank's life I was walking and talking to his rheumatologist about his condition and treatment on the way to Frank's ICU unit. She commented that we would have put our cat or dog to sleep by now and that these recent interventions were inhumane, really cruel and unusual.

By the end, I knew Frank's doctor was right. Advocating for Frank no longer meant following his wishes to an irrational conclusion. Advocating for my husband took on a greater meaning. I had to help him die.

Part Three

WIDOWHOOD

Funeral

THE NEXT MORNING, I PLANNED FOR FRANK'S funeral and autopsy. I felt as if I were going through the motions, disengaged from the gravity or implications of Frank's death. I had to detach to complete even the most basic tasks, tasks that would seem ordinary on any other day.

Frank had made two requests related to his funeral. He wanted to use a particular funeral home, and he wanted to give his medical practitioners an opportunity to learn more about scleroderma. Frank and I had a history with the funeral home, and I honored his request. My mother and three brothers had their wakes there, in addition to his father.

The day after Frank died, I met his daughters at the funeral home to arrange the wake, funeral, and burial. We selected a beautiful oak casket with da Vinci's Last Supper carved on both sides. We talked to the director about appointing a pastor, the obituary for the newspaper, and the prayer cards. The funeral director was caring and compassionate and made the process as straightforward as possible. Frank was an Air Force veteran, so we chose the local national cemetery with its meticulously attended grounds and special attention on holidays.

Among the many choices made in the funeral planning, we needed to choose the inscription for his headstone, with words that would capture his essence forever for visitors and passersby.

> *Man of strength*
> *and courage*
> *unconditional*
> *love and wisdom*

His second request was a little tougher for me. About a year earlier, Frank told me he wanted to give his medical practitioners the opportunity to gain insight about his disease from an autopsy since scleroderma was rare in the general population, especially among males. I promised him I would do this. This delayed his funeral for two weeks.

In that two-week interval, which seemed like an eternity, I took a four-day trip to the Lake of the Ozarks for my family's reunion. We had planned the trip and made deposits months in advance. I went through the motions of enjoying the reunion, but I missed Frank. He had been a part of every family gathering, and he had loved those events more than I did. Typically, the reunions were fun-filled and memorable, but my anticipation of his wake and funeral put a damper on the gathering.

I felt lousy on many levels, especially physically. I was fatigued. I thought I might have picked up a bug in the rehab center or hospital, so I made an appointment with my internist to see what was going on inside me. I was unclear about the characteristics of mononucleosis, but I figured my condition was close to it. He examined me, drew blood, and made the diagnosis of "grief." It was grief, only grief.

And the wake, funeral, and burial were still ahead.

We learned that the clergyman who married us had passed away, and I asked the funeral home director to recommend a female pastor to conduct the funeral. Before I left for the Lake of the Ozarks, I made arrangements for Pastor Penny Holste to meet me at home the evening I came back from the trip. When she did, I told her about Frank, his personality, his sense of humor, and his basic philosophy about life and his illness.

The autopsy was completed and the day for Frank's funeral services arrived. Pastor Penny put together a beautiful program and ceremony. Her message spoke of the hope and joy of Frank's life:

> "...If I had printed a title for my message today, it would be 'I Have a Plan' because Frank often used his engineer's mind and his creativity to devise new ways to solve problems. 'I have a plan' is a statement of hope that one can improve the present and make the future better and we see that hope in Frank.

> "...He said something like, 'Don't always ask why something happened but ask where is this leading me?'....It would be easy, after this goodbye, to ask why Frank had to die so young....But if we take Frank's advice, the better question is not 'Why' but 'Where is this leading us?'...We are not alone. God has a plan for our lives too, that we would bring joy to others—like Frank did— that we know joy ourselves once again."

Music played intermittently throughout the program, including "What a Wonderful World" by Louis Armstrong, the song we danced to at our wedding reception. The last song of the funeral was "Time to Say Good-Bye" by one of Frank's favorite artists, Sarah Brightman, whose voice he found especially comforting in the late stages of his illness.

During the service, I sat in the front pew to the right of the casket with other family members and my good friend, who was sitting next to me, holding my hand. I was trembling from sadness and fear of the unknown as Pastor Penny performed her portion of the program, awaiting my cue to move to the podium to do Frank's eulogy. I spoke with sadness but compartmentalized my emotions, as I was determined to get through it. My niece, Sherri, was my backup speaker, in the event I could not finish without breaking down. Beforehand, guests at the funeral questioned me about doing my husband's eulogy, but I wanted to be with him to support him in his journey to the physical end at the cemetery. I am often disappointed with eulogies, so to prevent a mundane or ineffective one, I planned what to say and pressed forward with it. During the rest of the funeral, my heart center was open and aching from the loss of my husband and best friend.

After the funeral ceremony at the mortuary's chapel, we proceeded to the cemetery for a brief service, which included Pastor Penny's reflections and a military gun salute to Frank. At the end of the service, two soldiers folded the flag from his casket and handed it to me in a silent and solemn moment.

Frank's Arms: Funeral

Finally, I made sure I was the last one to leave the cemetery chapel so I could be alone with Frank to give him a message. I walked up to the casket, patted it, and said, "Okay, I will wait to hear from you."

And I did hear from him three days later in the form of energy washing down my back and arms.

My Deal with Frank

WHEN FRANK SAID HE WAS SELFISH BECAUSE of his demands on me, I told him that was not so. I didn't like the idea that he thought he was selfish, so I came up with a plan to help him repay me. I offered to be his caregiver and advocate to the bitter end of his life, no matter what it took, if he would agree to be my advocate after he died. Then we sealed the deal with a "gentlemen's" handshake.

The impetus for this plan came from a social psychology principle called "the threat-to-self-esteem model." This model suggests that receiving help can sometimes pose a threat to someone's self-esteem. Recipients may resent help-givers and feel indebted if they are unable to return the favor in some way. A strategy to offset this threat is to give the person being helped a chance to repay. Indirectly, this action reinforces a person's dignity, and this aspect was most important to me when I made the deal with Frank as he fought his illness, dropped to 115 pounds, and coped with a feeding tube for nutrition and a diaper for bowel incontinence. I never begrudged him anything I had to do and was determined not to give him that impression. Generally, if conditions on help or judgments exist, the patient will sense that and feel "less than" as a result. People in our culture, especially men, highly value self-reliance and independence. I minimized his perception of dependence with teamwork. Frank and I assessed the problems and worked together on his setbacks and treatment goals.

He passed away two weeks after we made the deal. When he showed up in my bathroom three days after his funeral in an energetic form, I recognized he was keeping his part of the bargain to be my advocate. Frank was reaching out to me to let me know he was there for me.

Frank came to me multiple times after that first visit. I knew when he did because I felt sudden energy or chills on my arms and back. Most of the time, I felt his presence in the bathroom and kitchen and later in the basement. With my arms stretched out in a "hug me" position, I would often say aloud, "Frank, if that is you, hold me. Hold me." These seemingly random moments of energy and connection from Frank gave me great comfort. I was surprised at first but became accustomed to these interactions. I am glad he kept his word and has communicated to me in this way. These moments remind me of the movie *Ghost* with Demi Moore and Patrick Swayze. When Molly (Demi Moore) saw the apparition of Sam (Patrick Swayze) at the end of the movie, he said to her, "It's amazing, Molly. The love inside, you take it with you."

My romantic side wanted that to be true. I wanted to believe we exist in some form after we die and we get to take the love with us. I lost five brothers and a husband since *Ghost* was released. Each time I suffered the loss of a loved one, I fantasized my relatives would reach out to me the way Sam did in the film. I did not see Frank's apparition, but I sensed him in a way that felt real. My brothers came to me in the form of dreams after they died. I missed them and had hoped for some other kind of connection.

A part of me has subconsciously believed that the men in my life leave me. This sense of abandonment changed during a bodywork session in which I was working on grief and crying from the loss of Frank and my brothers. Then a heartwarming message came to me through the practitioner and my close friend, Deb Hall, to "find joy and comfort in the love they had for me." I scanned my memory for the sense of Frank and my brothers and recognized that each one loved me. I envisioned the twinkle in my brother Guy's eyes when he looked at me, even though he had died twenty years earlier. This new insight gave me immediate relief and some release from grief. I felt gratitude rather than loss and blessed that they could have taken that love with them and that they might still love me.

About a year and a half after Frank passed away, I noticed the light blinking on the phone one morning when I woke. I had not heard the phone ring. I pressed the button to hear the midnight message. Frank said his full name in his own voice. That was it. He was communicating with me with his name. I called my local phone carrier to see if I could save the message, and they indicated to me that I could not save it beyond two weeks. I wanted someone else to hear it because I assumed most people would not believe me. I was able to play it for my brother, Tom, and sister, Peggy, so I had witnesses. I wondered if the voicemail system malfunctioned and only picked up his first and last names and combined them from our greeting but Frank hadn't included his first name in the greeting. The system was not set up to simply state a name but to generate a full greeting. I decided that his message could not have come from a glitch in the voicemail.

Since I could not save the message, I taped it. I still have the tape with Frank saying his name. He left the same message two more times since that night: once when his children had visited and once on a weekend when I was particularly sad. For sentimental reasons, I have his voice on the phone's voicemail feature. Before he died, he created a recording on the voicemail for a caller to hear when there was no answer. The message says, "You have reached the ... residence, please leave a message after the beep." To keep his voice on this recording has cost me five dollars per month. Voices are important to me and I forget them over time, so the extra amount on my phone bill is worth it. I want to remember.

Frank reached out in other ways as well. One night, I was in our living room while watching a made-for-TV movie with Tom Selleck in the lead role as Jesse Stone. I was sitting in a chair adjacent to the sofa where Frank used to convalesce. Periodically, I looked over at the sofa and pictured Frank lying there. Sometime during the broadcast, I thought that we would have enjoyed this type of movie together. I was crying at the end of the movie because Jesse's dog died. A few seconds later, the ceiling fan in the living room made several slow rotations. The fan blades had no physical or logical reason to turn, and no draft or movement came through the living room or adjacent rooms. I had not moved from the chair. The fan had never rotated like that before. I knew at a gut level that Frank was with me. I knew I had to accept he was gone. I began to cry hysterically with bittersweet emotions. I was delighted he reached out to me and that he kept his end of the bargain, but it made me miss him more.

The ceiling fan periodically makes slow, inexplicable moves even now. The second time I noticed it, I sought a logical reason for the phenomenon. I'd had a new furnace and air conditioner installed, and I assumed the air from the duct was turning the fan blades until I noticed that the rotations continued after the furnace stopped and at times when the air was not blowing. When I had a hurtful experience with some friends, the same ceiling fan made slow rotations. Intuitively, I knew Frank was communicating his support to me again. In another instance, I was home with a cold for a few days, working on this memoir, when I walked to the front door, turned, and saw the fan moving slightly. I've ruled out all the logical reasons for these incidents, and Frank is the probable explanation.

Finally, I have wondered if he has fixed things around the house, like the toaster. I cannot prove this, of course. Some years back, the toaster was slowly dying and seemed to be near complete failure. It works now as if nothing was ever wrong. Frank was terrific at fixing broken things. He could take a motor apart and rebuild it without blueprints. Two of his jobs included maintaining equipment and troubleshooting during production down times. In upholding our deal, he could assist in making some minor repairs around the house. When something breaks, I appeal to him for a solution by asking for his help aloud. That doesn't always work, but it makes me feel better.

Frank's contact with me in multiple forms has helped me along in my grief, especially the ceiling fan incidents. We have honored our parts of the deal to take care of one another.

Frank still has his arms around me.

New Role as Widow

ONE DAY, FRANK WAS MY LIFE WITNESS. THE next, I was a widow. I had dedicated a great deal of my love and energy to my roles as wife, caregiver and advocate, especially in the final years of Frank's illness, and then they were gone.

I was numb.

I continued to suppress a flood of emotions. I had been focused on "fix this, fix that" for so long, that I forgot how to tune into my emotions or recognize them, especially the joyful moments in my life. I lived on mental autopilot and did not cultivate or express the feelings associated with my transition to widowhood. I experienced the tremendous loss of my husband and the subsequent loss of my previous roles, but you could not tell by my demeanor.

The grief had to manifest or bubble up in some way. Because I had not expressed sadness for my loss or my joy for the sweet memories of Frank, I continued to feel the loss in a state of chronic fatigue during the long and arduous process of grief. I was able to transcend the fatigue, at least superficially, pick up the pieces, and move on to other challenges. Eventually, I began to enjoy my solitude. My intensity, passion, and problem solving skills helped to some degree on the road to self-discovery and healing.

Deborah L. Phelps, Ph.D.

Whining has always been a way for me to release negative feelings. Admittedly, this is not the most adult behavior, but Frank tolerated it when the rest of my family and friends did not. Without Frank, I had no one to whom I could whine. Along with my husband, I lost part of my coping mechanism for suppressing emotions and tackling the challenges in life.

My position as an academic had the strongest impact on my adjustment from wife to widow because it was an integral part of my life and self-identity. During Frank's illness, many people wondered how I was able to juggle caregiving and my responsibilities as a faculty member and departmental chair, but my work gave me a sense of stability in contrast to the uncertainties associated with Frank's illness and death. I consistently had one more project to complete, one more report to write, one more stack of papers and exams to grade, one more committee meeting, one more board meeting to attend.

As a professor in human services and applied sociology, I watched as my students prospered and grew, knowing that I was training them to serve others. I was humbled as a number of them thanked me for the role I played in their lives and for the rippling effect my teaching had on their work experiences and the community. One of my alumni told me he had helped approximately 9,000 fathers improve their lives, fathers who support on average 2.5 children.

Academic activities outside the university also had a way of distracting me from my personal issues. One year after Frank's death, I joined the Association for Applied and Clinical Sociology (AACS) board and was invited to be the certification chair for the AACS, serving

Frank's Arms: New Role as Widow

the candidates who were interested in Certification as a Sociological Practitioner.

I continued to avoid my feelings and to delay processing the grief while I was pouring energy into my career. If I had not had a job and interactions with my colleagues and students, adjusting to widowhood would have been much more challenging. Aunt Betty's declaration that teaching was the noblest profession further validated my efforts.

Of course, my career as a coping mechanism could only get me so far. I focused on what I needed to do without thinking about it; I realized I needed to do self-discovery work. I understood my grief was bigger than I was and began therapy within a few months after Frank's death.

My therapist taught me to recognize emotions as they occurred and reassured me I felt more than I thought I did. I learned when I thought I was not feeling, I actually was. She guided me to reframe my experiences and responses to them and examine situations from different points of view. I learned I needed to allow myself to trust my natural grief process. I learned I was not going to return to "normal" after going through grief, and I recognized the need to move forward toward a "new normal." After about six months of therapy, I realized in one of the sessions that I had nothing else to discuss and that was my last session. Therapy moved me through my grief to a place where I was able to more easily exist beyond the grief and was valuable as a turning point in my self-awareness.

Nevertheless, the emotional suppression caught up with me about three years after Frank's death. I felt unusual symptoms, like pressure in my head and knew to check my blood pressure with the machine I had used to monitor Frank's readings. I developed high blood pressure. Twice, my systolic reading soared and that scared me. My blood pressure machine stops reading at a systolic pressure of 228; and twice, when the monitor was running, it moved beyond that level, read "error," and the cuff popped off my arm.

I tended to respond quickly to unusual physical manifestations, partially because of the close calls I experienced as Frank's advocate, and I had become hypersensitive to physical symptoms in myself. My internist prescribed medicines, yet they seemed ineffective, so he put me on six different ones in six weeks. The side effects, including arrhythmia and dehydration, were unsettling. I sought out the services of a cardiologist, but my hypertension became so erratic, he referred me to a blood pressure specialist. The specialist prescribed the right combination of medicines on my first visit. I continue to take these medications today.

My body had been out of balance for about six months, which was troubling. Though losing Frank was cataclysmic to my emotional well-being, his death followed myriad layers of unresolved grief. I'd lost five brothers, two aunts, a nephew, and two dogs over 15 years. It seemed that Frank's death triggered suppressed feelings I'd held from each of the previous losses. The weight of my grief finally surpassed my ability to contain it and manifested itself in unmanageable hypertension.

The message I received from this physical setback was to feel and express my feelings. I had heard these messages before, but sometimes I have to hear a message multiple times before I am ready to listen to it. Having severe hypertension was the "cosmic 2x4" I needed to wake me up to make some changes. I internalized the messages and acted on them.

Frank's Arms: New Role as Widow

I returned to therapy and focused on self-discovery work about my childhood. I needed guidance to understand the events of my childhood and to deal with my emotions and reactions. Over time and after a dinner conversation with a clinical psychologist friend, Mary Mondello, I realized that much of my emotional suppression came from my relationship with my father, who died of meningitis when I was 15 years old. As a rule, he did not allow his children to express anger toward him or question his motivations.

I took his actions personally and my perception of the situation was that he disapproved of me and I wasn't good enough, thus leaving me with a deep sense of vulnerability. I felt physically safe but unsafe on other levels. I now know that my father had not learned to express his emotions in a constructive manner because of his own traumatic childhood experiences.

When I was young, his words and actions taught me to stuff my feelings deep down inside and forget about them. His style of expressing his emotions and oppressing mine laid the foundation for my denial and skill at compartmentalization. I needed a long time to understand the dynamics underlying this issue. After some enlightening information about my father's childhood and many self-care activities, I was able to partially complete this unfinished business even though I'm unsure if anyone ever fully processes childhood experiences.

Despite the difficulties in my childhood relationships, my family of origin served as an anchor as I moved into widowhood. The importance of extended family became apparent during my struggles, and I revitalized relationships that had diminished because of the demands from

Frank's illness. If not for my family members, coping would have been more difficult. It was reassuring to know they were there for me and I could call or meet them.

At the time of Frank's death, I had five siblings living near me. One sister, Georgian, drove me to his funeral service and stayed with me the first night after the funeral. Other siblings and extended family members (nieces, nephews, cousins, and in-laws) visited me and invited me to events and dinners. Their unconditional love and support helped and comforted me as I grew in my new role.

My blended family members had a positive impact on being a widow. By comforting and supporting Frank's three loving and generous daughters, I helped myself. His children needed a great deal of attention and support in the loss of their father. Frank was their "rock," and they regarded him highly. His daughters and I kept in contact with one another more frequently when I became a widow. Over time, our contact has diminished as we all have had exceedingly busy lives with our jobs and their children's activities. On the first anniversary of Frank's death, we went to breakfast at his favorite restaurant, reminisced about Frank, and then visited his gravesite where we shared more stories and talked to him. The four of us met like this on the first few anniversaries of Frank's death. Our dialogue helped us adjust as we chatted among ourselves and talked to Frank. I served as their link to their father, and they served as mine to my husband. During these encounters, I could see Frank in each of them: their looks, their mannerisms. I knew that part of Frank still lived.

Besides family, my other anchor was a solid and supportive group of friends. I drew near to my friends who were thoughtful, loving, and giving. Each of them came over individually and then together to visit and bring me food after his death. On my first birthday as a widow, several friends gave me the royal treatment, which included food, a foot massage, foot soak, and a body massage with other gifts. Two of my friends were widows, which gave us a common bond. We were part of a sisterhood one can join only upon enduring the loss of a beloved spouse. One has to experience it to understand it, and the three of us shared that. My widow friends helped me establish myself in my new role.

But I had some unhappy times in my relationships with my family and friends. I learned the big lesson that I, alone, was responsible for taking myself out of loneliness. Sometimes, I reached out to friends and family and got the message that I was on my own. I told them I was lonely and the loneliness was unbearable at times, and I got little response. I began to think people were cold, callous, and insensitive. I was losing faith in humanity because they stopped supporting me and my cries of loneliness. One friend said, "You are on your own," making it clear that my loneliness was my problem to solve. I did not understand their reactions for a long time and became disillusioned and disenchanted.

I eventually understood that we all bring a certain amount of "baggage" to our relationships from our personal perspectives and individual experiences. These experiences influence our perceptions and reactions to the loss of a spouse. We can take on only so much of other people's grief and pain, and I might have pushed people too far. Not every friend or family member was able to deal with me as I moved through my grief. I think part of the dynamic was that most people in my social world had not experienced widowhood, so when I vented about my predicament, they were at a loss for words, confused about how to respond to me, or overwhelmed with my situation.

As I moved firmly into my role as widow, I recognized we keep some relationships and move out of others. I struggled as I began to lose friendships, partially because "letting go" has always been a challenge. I tried to make sense of my widowhood and the loss of friendships and am still not completely sure why some friendships waned or friends did not respond.

Perhaps we drifted apart.

Perhaps their lack of response was a gift—a gift to teach me to find the answers within and to move independently through my grief with the reward of self-discovery.

It is more difficult for me to let go when I don't understand something, and I typically ruminate until I have clarity. I received an insightful message by e-mail one morning that led me to "trust the process" and allow the unresolved questions about my relationships to remain: "Whenever something doesn't work out the way you thought it would, instead of thinking that something went wrong, see it as something that went unexpectedly well, but for reasons that are not yet apparent. Everything plays to your favor." (©Mike Dooley, www.tut.com)

While I attempted to let go of old relationships, I did keep some friends and I made new ones, which helped alleviate the sadness from the loss of others. Creating new friendships was a challenge but one that I overcame with effort and perseverance. These new relationships are based on who I am now.

Avenues for Escape

WHILE THERAPY, HYPERTENSION, AND MY job were getting my attention, I was planning avenues for escape from my grief and loneliness. I couldn't outrun those conditions, but I tried. People often commented that I knew how to take care of myself, because I took risks and went on adventures. One of my widow friends, Malinda, referred to me as "first lady" because I introduced her to many new activities. One could question, however, if I was taking care of myself or running from loss.

In the first few years after Frank died, I spent a great deal of time away from my home. A tremendous hurdle for me was to learn to live alone and not to feel lonely. On average, I saw movies twice a week. Sometimes, I saw the same movie multiple times. On the weekends, I often left my house in the morning and did not come back for 12 to 14 hours. I became a master at staying lost in a crowd. A typical day might be breakfast out, shopping, lunch, one or two movies, and maybe dinner. I found countless ways to stay away from home because I wanted to avoid an empty house.

Weekends were the loneliest times for me as I journeyed through widowhood. I found Friday nights to be particularly difficult since I thought of it as a couples' night. Without Frank, Fridays after work became painful.

Rather than going home from work, I went to a movie, where I sat in the dark and got lost in the plot.

In my adventures away from home, I didn't particularly like going to indoor malls because couples and families stood out to me. I imagined that every couple and family in the malls was happy. The positive energy, along with the smell of the pretzels, cookies, restaurants, and especially men's cologne, stirred up the longings in me for companionship and family. My lot as a widow was obvious.

I read countless novels to escape, mostly suspense or serial killer novels. I often finished a novel in one or two days, especially James Patterson's books. Slowly, after those first few years of my widowhood, the novels and movies tapered, and I became more content at home alone. I learned that escape through novels, movies, and running errands helped temporarily. These mini-escapes served as short-term distractions from my grief and solitude, which still existed when I returned home. I had to learn to deal with the pain through other means.

Travel was a great gift that was intertwined with Frank's death, but it became an obstacle in my adjustment to widowhood. Six weeks after Frank's death, I took a widow trip for a week as a reward to myself for all the hard work in caregiving. I picked Vancouver, British Columbia. A work colleague gave Vancouver rave reviews for a cosmopolitan place with beautiful scenery, and I had spent little time in the northwest. My sister, Kathy, agreed to go to support me in my grief. Her husband was accommodating about it because he cared a great deal for Frank. We stayed at first-class hotels and spared no expense. I bought myself an expensive winter coat at an upscale hotel, which was more than I had ever spent on a coat. We went shopping, sightseeing, dining, and to Victoria Island. The scenery was breathtaking, especially on the ferry from the mainland. This trip helped by giving me distance from home and Frank's death and it served as a distraction. Time and space helped me to continue to adjust to the loss.

Later on in my widowhood, I made a trip to Maui with my sister, Peggy, and a good friend, which was another delightful step on my road to recovery. We went to a luau, shopped, ate great food, took the road trip to Hana, and got body massages, and a hot bath. The sound and smells of the ocean were peaceful and wonderful. We stopped at a roadside restaurant and ate fish caught by local boat captains who were identified on the menu. For the last night of the trip, we stayed at a luxury hotel on the beach and reveled in the first-class service. The music, lights, and beach were inspirational. We all sensed a depth in spirit and were enriched by the experience.

In addition, I made a number of trips to visit my aunt in Phoenix, Arizona, and drove up to Sedona for self-discovery. I often traveled with friends and family, rented houses in Sedona, and was eager to learn and embrace its surprises. Sedona was always spiritually and emotionally uplifting. I opened myself to opportunities and messages. We hiked, received bodywork, and soaked up the wonderful energy from the vortexes. We had deep and meaningful conversations related to personal growth.

Some of the trips were difficult.

Ten days after my widow trip to Vancouver, I took a regional jet to a work-related conference in Philadelphia. The flight to Vancouver was smooth and easy, but the flight to Philadelphia was turbulent. Maybe I should not have taken a week's vacation and then turned around a short time later to go to an out-of-town conference while my grief was so raw. I was so tired at the conference that I only had enough energy to take a shower and ride the elevator down to the meeting room, where I dropped into a chair. My emotional fatigue had caught up with me. I didn't have the wherewithal to participate in the conference as I normally would have. I sat and watched people talk. I could hear and see them talking, but I was too tired to process their information. I left the conference early and flew standby to get back home as soon as possible. I do not think I was ever that driven to get home. The damage had been done to my psyche. I remained uneasy with flying for several years, and I went to great lengths to avoid regional jets.

Overcoming my fear of flying began slowly. About a year after the Philadelphia trip, I flew to Detroit for a conference and had a seemingly chance experience with a stranger. We had changed our seat assignments at the last minute and ended up sitting next to one another on the 90-minute flight.

She was an angel sent to help me deal with my fear of flying.

She had been through a similar difficulty but had managed to work through her fear. She shared that she used to have so much fear that she would go to the airport and not get on the plane. I drilled her with doubtful questions about every aspect of uncertainty in flying: air, turbulence, pilots, regional jets, take-off and landing, dropping fast, and all sorts of questions that could generate a shaky mindset for a passenger. She responded with reassuring answers and shot holes into all my concerns and arguments. She recommended tranquilizers before a flight and other remedies.

After the trip to Detroit, I meditated to figure out why I was afraid and realized I associated flying with Frank's death because of the short time interval between his death and the turbulent flight to Philadelphia. On the subsequent flights, I was reliving his death each time I flew. By associating flying with Frank's death, I developed a sense of loss of control each time I got on a plane.

In April 2008, I went to a graduate alumni reunion in New Haven, Connecticut. A nor'easter off the coast compounded my apprehension of flying as I was making my way back to Saint Louis. Watching the news did not help my emotional state, as the weather forecasters kept announcing the storm was coming and that it had arrived. The rain and wind pounded my car as I drove from New Haven to Bradley International Airport in Hartford. I couldn't believe planes were going to fly in that weather, let alone I might get on one. At the airport, I changed my flight so I could avoid a regional jet even though it meant I had to fly through Dallas rather than take a direct flight home. Even with the large plane, bad turbulence affected it. At one point during the flight the pilot announced, "I am trying to find smooth air!" That was all I needed to hear! Of course, we landed safely, but I felt anxious the entire time.

Nevertheless, I overcame my fear after a flight to Jacksonville, Florida, in October of that year with the help of two friends who comforted me and walked me through the unavoidable regional jet flights. This was a big breakthrough for me and such a relief to experience my fear of flying lift.

I developed several other coping mechanisms for flying during my fearful phase. As recommended by the stranger on my Detroit flight and by my primary physician, I took anti-anxiety medicine while flying for much of the time I was having trouble. The medicine relaxed me and made it so I could get to my destination without being overcome by fear. I developed a trick of picturing people who were comfortable on an airplane in miniature form and imagined them sitting on my shoulder, knee, or in the seat pocket, whenever I experienced turbulence. When I did this, it helped me visualize and internalize their calmness. My other comforting technique was to imagine angels sitting in every empty seat, positioned in the cockpit, and holding up the wings. I no longer need the medication when I fly although I still picture the angels. Overcoming my fear of flying meant I was moving forward with my life. I was adjusting to the loss of Frank and embracing being a widow. Flying was a symbol of fear in deep grief and one of release in recovery from the despair.

In addition to recreational diversion and traveling, I received massages and engaged in energy work as much as possible to help me cope more fully with my grief and move strongly into my new role as a widow. My massage school had a policy of allowing graduates unlimited free student massages, and I took advantage of that opportunity with as many as four per month. Cindy Goodnetter, the massage school owner and a good friend, looked out for me in my grief. During a phone conversation, she said, "Where are you right now? Drive to the school and get on the table." Many times when I was getting massages, I would think to myself, "I must be living right" or "I am being treated like a queen." Massage, as a form of touch, was reassuring and loving. It relaxed, rejuvenated, and refreshed me.

Sometimes I was so relaxed from the massage that I could not drive home immediately afterward. Massage also improved my physical health. Ultimately, it lowered my heart rate, breath rate, and blood pressure. It relaxed muscles and increased blood flow. My muscles became more flexible and toned.

Energy and bodywork continued to have a profound effect on my well-being. I worked with the healing modalities that I had started while Frank was ill, including Reiki, Craniosacral Therapy, and Healing Touch. Periodically, I gave people treatments, knowing that as you give, you receive. This is especially true in Reiki: the energy that transfers from the practitioner into the client returns directly and indirectly.

Another activity that helped me in overcoming my grief was to listen to guided meditations. I had used meditations by Billie Topa Tate while Frank was ill and was familiar and comfortable with her voice and imagery. She has one meditation in particular that I found eased my grief. She guides the participant to picture loved ones, look into their eyes, and send love to their hearts. Through her instructions, I imagined energy coming down from the divine center of Frank and pictured a blanket of golden light surrounding, protecting, and comforting him. I finished the meditations by telling Frank good-bye and that I would see him again. This practice helped me to gradually let go of Frank and to progress as a widow.

Someone told me that you can live without a spouse or loved one but not without community. I believe the Holy Spirit or some equivalent had a hand in my new ventures to give me a stronger sense of community. I became more religious after Frank died and attended church more frequently, which gave me deeper connections and more grounding. As I connected more, I feared less and became more secure. I volunteered to be a member of my parish council and was elected to be the chair of the council for a four-year period.

Another avenue that I chose to boost my healing and to deepen my spirituality was to begin "association" with the Sisters of St. Joseph of Carondelet, a group of Catholic sisters based in Saint Louis who came to the United States in 1836 to work with deaf children. They are a fabulous group of women who embody a "charism" of unifying love, which is manifested in "serving the dear neighbor without distinction." Their platform is one of gentleness, peace, and joy, and their ministry has survived over the centuries. My knowledge about the association came seemingly by chance when I flew with three of the sisters to New Jersey for a former dean and friend's inauguration as a college president. I signed up and began my journey of blessings with them. I knew I needed a more solid sense of community since I was primarily alone, and felt that joining this group would give me that solidity. Moreover, I believed in their philosophy, witnessed their grace, and felt safe and comfortable joining them in association as a way to give back.

As part of the process to become an associate, I took classes about the history and principles of the sisters twice a month for a year. Currently, my training cohort, Rita's Rascals, meets every month to pray, reflect, and share the state of our hearts (our emotional state of being). We listen lovingly and purposefully. The sisters and my fellow associates pray for me on an ongoing basis. I can sense the loving energy from the group and the purity of their hearts when I interact with them. They "walk the walk" in taking care of those in need and do not judge or exclude anyone. This level of support is rewarding and anchoring. My membership in association with the sisters and with the parish council have expanded my interpersonal relationships and enriched my quality of life.

Moreover, I participated in a number of workshops, including ones on grief, to learn more ways to process my own. Over the years, I attended events on death and dying, which were held at funeral homes and conference centers. Topics included caregiving, widowhood, and mourning. The workshops gave me insight and clarity about my experiences and reinforced my belief that I was not alone; others had endured what I had with similar processes and outcomes. I consistently embraced opportunities for growth and understanding about my experiences and reactions to death and loss.

I grew personally from a creative nonfiction-writing workshop at a local university. The workshop helped in a number of ways, one of which was to serve as the inspiration to write this memoir. My experiences with the fellow students, some of whom were writing professionals, gave me confidence in my abilities and insight into the writing process. We critiqued each other's written work, and I was able to hold my own within the group. We had writing homework assignments, and on one occasion, I wrote an essay about Frank's illness. The instructor and students encouraged me to enlarge the essay into a book.

Overall, I tried various ways to escape and heal as I moved through my grief and into widowhood. I had some setbacks along the way, but they were just that: setbacks and building blocks for wisdom.

Transition into Singlehood

I BEGAN TO THINK OF MYSELF AS "SINGLE" rather than "widow."

This conscious shift came in the spring of 2013 and was reinforced when I attended the conference of the Association of Colleges of Sisters of St. Joseph (ACSSJ). I paid attention to the term "single" as other people used it. Some referred to themselves as single when in between relationships even if they had never married. I decided to view myself as single and to introduce myself that way because the term "widow" denoted loss and sadness. Nevertheless, I sometimes introduce myself as a widow out of habit and must do so on forms that ask for my marital status.

During the first evening's dinner at the ACSSJ conference, one of the Sisters said, "With the term 'widow', one's identity is tied up in loss rather than gain." This motivated me further to shift my attitude toward one of abundance in singlehood.

The ACSSJ conference focused on developing a "new consciousness," which solidified my re-identification as single. At the conference we talked about ideas I had read about and discussed. I had heard messages, such as "get out of your own way," "be mindful," and "be present and in the now." I had been working on these concepts and knew what they meant, but hearing them in the conference setting brought them home in a way that I needed to hear at that moment in transitioning to my new role. I recognized that I needed to become "present" in singlehood. I had to be in the present or be lost in the past.

One of my colleagues in my writing group asked me if I had a turning point in my grief. I cannot identify just one. The process formally began when I conducted rituals in Frank's honor. During the first Christmas season after his death, I went into the living room and lit candles and said prayers in his honor. This helped in the process of confirming his death and letting go. His birthday, Christmas, New Year's, and our wedding anniversary were all within a two-week period. The close timing of these events intensified my grief, but I was able to deal with many of these important family holidays in a short time rather than experiencing them throughout the year.

The activities and support came together for me with gradual change. I noticed I was moving from grief and loss when I began to move framed pictures of Frank. For example, I moved the wedding picture from the side of my bed to the upstairs. Now pictures of him are on a bookcase in the basement of my home. I moved pictures at my computer station at work to the bookcases behind my desk. I began to visit his grave on the other side of town less often, although I sometimes made a special trip on holidays and when I was in the area. When I visited, I talked to Frank and kissed his grave marker.

Frank's arms were wrapped around the experiences I had along the way in marriage, sickness, death, widowhood, and singlehood. He has had a lasting impact on me spiritually, mentally, emotionally, and physically.

Conclusion

AT THE TIME OF THIS WRITING, I AM MAKING dinner for two of my sisters and their husbands. I can see Frank in everything I do, including my methods in preparing the meal systematically, just one of the many profound impacts Frank had on me.

Yes, I have a longing in my heart because he is no longer here in his physical form. But I am comforted by the suggestion from the movie *Powder* (1995) that Frank might not have gone but could have become part of "everything" instead, including me.

Three scenes in *Powder* offer an alternative understanding of loneliness and reinforce the idea that when a person dies, he or she is not gone. In one scene, Sean Flanery's character, Jeremy "Powder" Reed, said: "Inside most people, there is a feeling of being separate, separated from everything, and they are not. They are part of absolutely everyone and everything."

In a later scene, Powder reassured Lance Henriksen's character, police chief Doug Barnum, about the death of his spouse: "She didn't go someplace. Your wife. I felt her go—not away—just out. Everywhere."

Finally, when Powder was struck by lightning, he was energized by it, died, and merged with the horizon. Immediately his energy swept back and through the lead characters who watched his death. They became exhilarated and joyful when Powder's energy passed through them.

I'm also encouraged by the message from my bodywork session to find comfort in the fact that Frank loved me and from *Ghost* that he might have taken that love with him.

I've been weary during my journey through caregiving and widowhood and, at the same time, hopeful and inspired. I was steadfast in my roles as caregiver and advocate while taking care of myself. Coping with the circumstances of illness, death, and widowhood was difficult, but I learned invaluable lessons and developed an appreciation for the opportunities that lie in uncertainty.

Even with the supportive messages from movies, therapy sessions, personal relationships, religious and spiritual experiences, workshops, and bodywork and energy sessions, I still experience loneliness and sadness.

As I complete this memoir, part of me doesn't want to let it go because it represents letting go of Frank, as I did incrementally with revisions of this work and in coming to the end of this chapter. Many writers have spoken about gaining self-awareness through writing. I'm partial to Flannery O'Connor's statement: "I write to discover what I know." (Fitzgerald, 1979). This has certainly been true for me while bringing my thoughts to the surface and coming to terms with loss.

No matter how one faces loss, release of the pain occurs in layers, as healing takes place.

Part Four

REFLECTIONS

Things I Wish I Had Known

When I began writing this memoir, I wanted to include a catchall chapter to cover the lessons and insights I learned along the way that didn't fall neatly into my story. With hindsight, I wish I had known many things at the start of Frank's diagnosis, whether it was specifically about the illness or the impact the years of illness would have on our lives. I hope these reflections help you avoid some challenges and heartache.

I wish I had known about the diagnosis and prognosis of scleroderma despite the fact that Frank defied the odds. If we had caught the scleroderma earlier, he might have been a candidate for an intervention, such as stem cell replacement and possibly a cure. Even though the cause and cure of scleroderma have yet to be discovered, familiarity with the medical literature might have given me more clarity and comfort.

I wish I had known more about the biggest threats to Frank's physical stability and deterioration. I did learn that infection was to be avoided. I shifted into hypervigilance to protect him by keeping myself well and preventing him from being subjected to others who might have a contagious condition, such as, a cold or flu. In addition, I got a flu shot every fall to keep from getting sick. Now, if someone meets me and does not tell me he or she is contagious, I consider withholding that information rude. I need to be able to decide whether to postpone the meeting to keep myself healthy.

I wish I had known about the possible symptoms Frank might develop; this knowledge could have prepared me for the physical impairments or setbacks that occurred. This information should be more readily available from the literature, the Internet, or a medical provider.

I wish I had known more about side effects from the pharmaceuticals prescribed and contraindicated foods. Knowledge is power and can ease the patient's physical discomfort. Enduring the progression of a terminal illness is bad enough without unfortunate or avoidable complications. We could have spared Frank unnecessary agony.

I wish I had known about the practical applications of health care policy, such as a living will. As long as Frank could speak for himself, he could change the dimensions of it. If this situation happened again, I would be ready and able to prevent some of the chaos and disorganization. Most likely, I would wait to create the living will until Frank's death was imminent. Theoretically that could result in fewer changes to his health care, making the treatment plan easier to implement. I realize waiting to create the living will contradicts conventional guidance. People are encouraged to create a living will when they are healthy and have mental clarity. In theory, this provides loved ones and medical practitioners the direction needed to execute a patient's intentions. However, I knew my husband and suspect we moved on this matter too early. As with most aspects of illness and death, there is no single correct answer.

I wish I had known I would have one income for most of my adult life, due partially to Frank's illness. Both of us lost income for a decade at different times in our relationship. I would have engaged in more creative financial planning from the outset of our marriage.

I wish I had known how to prepare for the loneliness in widowhood and the process of pulling myself out of loneliness. I needed years to feel comfortable in my solitude and, more recently, in the company of a shelter cat, named Powder.

I wish I had known more about life after death: what form we take and how long we hang around in spirit form. I would have been more prepared to respond to Frank's contact. Awareness is the first step to understanding and acceptance.

Other Caregiving Insights

ONE CAREGIVING LESSON I LEARNED WAS that physicians in training can be kept out of the patient's hospital room or unit. Because Frank was in a teaching hospital, medical students, residents, and fellows of various specialties checked on him. Those doctors in training frequently shadowed the attending physicians to learn by observation and discussion of a "real" patient's course of illness. Typically, after the attending physician finished his visit, they imitated the exam, checked Frank's vital signs, and listened to his heart and lungs. Sometimes, when they were waiting outside his unit to examine him, I felt uncomfortable, partially because of the frequency of encounters we had with them. Many times, they stood in the hall, presumably eager to learn more about a patient with a rare illness. Frank was good natured about the repeated examinations, but I saw the situation from a different perspective. During one hospitalization, a nurse sensed my unease with the trainees and she told me they could be kept out of his hospital room. I took advantage of that on occasion to give Frank and me some relief and space from medical contact.

On a similar topic, I learned through studies that physicians can be fired. We had no occasion to do this, but this insight was reassuring during his health care.

As I mentioned in the "Infected Stitch" chapter, mutual participation with the medical practitioner in one's health care is beneficial to the patient and caregivers. I learned in graduate school from reading and discussing physicians' perspectives, such as, Francis Peabody's in *The Care of the Patient* and Ray Duff's in *"Close-up" versus "Distant" Ethics* patients are more likely to get better and stay better if they actively participate in their health care and if physicians listen to their patients. These ideas were reinforced as I participated in Frank's treatment. Some great doctors listened to him, including his rheumatologist and cardiologists. They respected him and attended to his point of view, even though they knew he minimized the gravity of his illness.

Part of mutual participation is the idea that asking questions will most likely have a positive effect on the outcome. Theoretically, the more questions you ask, the better the care will be, partially because of the complex and complicated "sociopolitics" in the healthcare system and the importance in understanding the diagnosis and treatment plan as I have addressed in the medical intervention chapters.

Patient advocates are important in health care, especially when a patient is in the hospital. Advocacy can positively affect the treatment outcome and may prevent medical mistakes in the hospital, which come in many forms. In medical sociology, these mistakes are referred to as nosocomial (occurring while in the hospital) and iatrogenesis (illness caused by a health care provider). If the patient goes alone, patient advocates are typically on the hospital staff. The "take home" message is to avoid going to the hospital alone and to obtain advocacy from the hospital if necessary.

Frank's Arms: Other Caregiving Insights

Caregivers also need support and advocacy for the emotional and physical strain that occurs in the process of caring for the patient. The caregiver would theoretically be stronger and more effective in practice not "to go it alone." Benefits from asking for help and ideally, offers of help, are priceless. Silent companionship, a phone call, gift, or any act of kindness in support could go a long way in assisting those who care for others. In addition, there are endless opportunities for self-care available to the seeker.

Epilogue

As I labored over the edits to this book, I took a break for lunch and visited Dressel's, the site of my first date with Frank.

When I walked into the restaurant, I felt nothing.

I was seated and faced the direction where Frank and I laughed and talked thirty years earlier. It was early in the lunch hour and the only other customer on my side of the restaurant was a man who sat with his back to the wall, facing me; he was seated near the table I'd once shared with Frank. The sounds of jazz filled the restaurant. I smelled wood, a hint of beer, fried food, and a signature dish of Dressel's, homemade Bavarian chips.

Memories stirred and my emotions surged.

When my server brought my lunch – a burger – I asked her about the layout and history of Dressel's; I took notes on a takeout menu. I learned that John Dressel, the first owner, actively wrote poetry and the pub gave him the freedom to write and the environment to celebrate it before he transferred ownership to his son, Ben.

The walls of the first floor were covered with framed photographs of writers, musicians, plays, operas and John's poetry, producing an artsy, intelligent atmosphere.

After I finished my burger, which was as good as I remembered it, I asked permission to look at the second floor to see if the surroundings triggered other memories. Upstairs featured Gaslight Square, a historic St. Louis landmark. I was struck by the connections in my life that seemed to create a circle: the history of St. Louis tied to the history of the restaurant, tied to my first date with Frank, and ultimately, tied to the journey recorded in my memoir.

Glossary

Note: Unless indicated, all definitions are mine. Dorland refers to *Dorland's Illustrated Medical Dictionary* (2012). Sell et al. refers to the *Dictionary of Medical Terms,* Sixth Edition (2013).

A

abdominal surgery: surgery with a sizable incision in the abdominal area

active euthanasia: deliberate action by another to end a person's life, e.g., lethal injections or overdose of pills

advocacy: pleading the cause of another, in this case for a patient

anesthesiologist: a physician or dentist specializing in anesthesiology (Dorland)

anesthesia: the loss of the ability to feel pain caused by the administration of a drug or by other medical interventions, often administered in surgery (Dorland)

Angel Repair Workshops: group energy or bodywork exclusively with my friends; a name that we gave our sessions

anti-anxiety medicine: helps to reduce anxiety or apprehension, e.g., Ativan, Xanax

assisted suicide: assisting someone to commit suicide; also known as mercy killing or euthanasia

Association of Colleges of the Sisters of St. Joseph (ACSSJ): an association of nine colleges and universities that follow the educational mission of the Sisters of St. Joseph. Fosters collaboration among all the member institutions, provides resources for faculty, staff, and students, and encourages mission integration on each campus. For more information: http://www.acssj.org/

autoimmune disorders: disorders marked by an abnormality in the immune system causing the production of antibodies which work against one's own tissues and other body materials. Examples are scleroderma, lupus, and rheumatoid arthritis (Sell et al.)

autopsy: examination of a body after death, using dissection, to determine the cause of illness (Sell et al.)

B

bile ducts: ducts in which bile passes from the liver or gallbladder to the upper part of the intestines (duodenum)

biopsy: the removal and examination of tissue from the living body to establish a precise diagnosis (Dorland)

bodywork: a generic term for treatment to the body in the form of complementary or alternative medicine, e.g., massage or craniosacral therapy

C

cardiac arrest: sudden cessation of cardiac output and blood circulation; the heart stops beating (Sell et al.)

cardiac intensive care (CIC): intensive care unit for patients with heart problems

cardiological electrophysiologist: physician who specializes in placing and monitoring defibrillators and pacemakers; combination units are referred to as AICD units

cardiopulmonary resuscitation (CPR): emergency procedure, consisting of external cardiac massage and artificial respiration (heart and lung); used as the first treatment for a person who has collapsed, is unresponsive, has no pulse, and has stopped breathing. The purpose is to restore blood circulation and prevent death or brain damage due to the lack of oxygen (Sell et. al.)

caregiving: giving care to another person; in this case, the one who is sick

charism: philosophy of the Sisters of St. Joseph of Carondelet to serve the dear neighbor without distinction (everybody) and to depict unifying love and reconciliation

chemotherapy: The treatment of a disease by chemical agents; applied to harm or kill disease-causing microorganisms. All of these agents have side effects, the most common of which are nausea and vomiting, suppression of bone marrow function, and hair loss. (Sell et al.)

compartmentalization: to separate one's emotions into an isolated compartment

computed tomography (CT): a method for examining the body's soft tissues using x-rays with the beam passing repeatedly through a body part. A CT can detect tumors, fluid buildup, dead tissue, and other abnormalities. (Sell et al.)

congestive heart failure: abnormal condition with circulatory congestion and fluid buildup in the lungs. (Sell et al.)

Costa, Sue: a practitioner and teacher who specializes in CranioSacral therapy, SomatoEmotional Release, and Lymphatic Drainage. On sabbatical.

Craniosacral Therapy: type of bodywork developed by John Upledger and taught through The Upledger Institute. Designed to enhance body functioning and alleviate pain and discomfort. Stimulates the client's own natural healing. Used for physical, emotional, mental, and spiritual difficulties. For more information: www.upledger.com

D

dialysis: medical procedure for filtering waste products from the blood of patients with kidney disease. (Sell et al.)

do not resuscitate (DNR): a directive to withhold resuscitation for cardiac arrest (not to revive a person whose heart and/or breathing has stopped), allowing for a natural death. (Sell et al.)

E

emergency medical technician (EMT): professional trained in prehospital care for the sick or injured. Typically limited to life support intervention and transportation to a medical treatment center

emergency room (ER): hospital unit in which persons with acute physical and mental conditions go for treatment often as a transition to hospital admission

endotracheal tube: a breathing tube used during surgery to assist the patient in breathing. It is generally inserted after the anesthesia starts to take effect and is removed when the patient can safely breathe, typically as he or she is becoming aware (FGTA Research)

energy work: a generic term for complementary or alternative medicine, which directs energy to a client or manipulates the energy field to promote harmony or balance, e.g., Reiki or Pranic Healing

extubation: removal of an endotracheal tube

F

feeding tube: extends from a machine outside of the patient, which is designed to transfer liquid food directly into the stomach ("G" tube) or to the small intestine ("J" tube)

G

Goodnetter, Cindy: a healer and teacher who founded A Gathering Place Wellness Education Center. The center promotes health and well-being with massage and energy/body work services, massage therapy programs, continuing education classes, and community outreach. For more information: http://www.agatheringplace.com/

grief: pattern of responses, physical or emotional (proceeding from disbelief or denial to anger and guilt to final acceptance of the loss of a loved one) (Sell et al.)
Elisabeth Kübler-Ross developed stages of grief and wrote several books on death, dying, and grief. For more information on her books: http://www.ekrfoundation.org/

guided meditation: popular form of meditation with guided imagery, commonly conducted with the use of CDs or other electronic means. Guided meditations are also held with healers in various venues. For more information: http://msi-healing.com/our-story/billie-topa-tate

H

Hall, Deb: a healer and teacher in bodywork who offered a variety of healing modalities, including massage and craniosacral therapy; currently in retirement

Healing Touch: type of alternative healing using hands-on and energy-based techniques to balance and align the human energy field. The Healing Touch practitioner reactivates the mind-body connection to eliminate blockages to self-healing (Sell et al.). For more information: http://www.genesis-aplacetoheal.com/Healing%20Touch.htm

Henwood, Kerry: an internationally recognized integrative healer, inspirational speaker and teacher. Uses a variety of modalities, including sound to support healing. For more information: http://www.shamanicgrace.com/

I

iatrogenic mistakes: mistakes as a result of medical care that causes illness or health problems

integrated breath session: utilization of a circular breathing technique, facilitated by Tom Tessereau, Executive Director of the Healing Arts Center and adapted from Judith Kravitz's Transformational Breath modality. Described as conscious breath work that facilitates natural healing and greater physical, mental and spiritual health. For more information: https://www.thehealingartscenter.com/ or http://www.transformationalbreath.com/

intensive care unit (ICU): hospital unit in which patients with life-threatening conditions have constant care and close monitoring (Sell et al.)

intubation: placement of a tube into an opening (Sell et al.)

K

Karuna Reiki (Reiki of compassion): the symbols and intentions are complementary to Usui Reiki. For more information: http://www.reiki.org/karunareiki/karunahomepage.html

L

laparoscopy: an operation within the abdominal cavity using a laparoscope (a type of endoscope) introduced through a small incision in the abdominal wall (Sell et al.)

Law of Least Effort: one of the laws developed by Deepak Chopra in his *Seven Spiritual Laws of Success*. Recommends we accept people, situations, and events as they occur; take responsibility for our situations and for all events seen as problems; relinquish the need to defend our point of view. (Chopra Center) For more information: http://www.chopra.com/sslos

Living Insights Center: a religious and spiritual center that regards all persons as sacred and honors all religious/spiritual traditions. Offers sanctuaries, classes, and energy/bodywork sessions. Reported that miracles have occurred at the foot of the statue of St. Therese, the little flower. Open to the public. For more information: http://www.livinginsights.com/

lupus: chronic autoimmune disease of unknown cause, affecting women more frequently than men. (Sell et al.)

M

magnetic resonance imaging (MRI): imaging technique using a magnetic field to view internal systems. Useful for imaging soft tissue (Sell et al.)

massage therapy: manipulation of the soft tissue of the body through rubbing, stroking, kneading, or gripping to improve muscle tone, relax the person, or improve circulation (Sell et al.)

meditation: relaxing and surrendering in silence. Commonly based on Buddha's teaching that answers or clarity come from silence. Also, use of guided meditations with imagery

N

nasogastric tube: tube passed into the stomach through the nose used to aspirate (withdraw) stomach contents or secretions or to facilitate nasogastric feeding (Sell et. al.)

nosocomial mistakes: mistakes that occur within the hospital setting, e.g., staff infections or falling out of bed

P

pacemaker-defibrillator: combination unit with a pacemaker and defibrillator placed in the chest (AICD unit). The pacemaker portion of the unit paces the heart for good rhythm; the defibrillator shocks the heart when it slows or stops

passive euthanasia: withholding treatment or medical intervention and allowing the patient to die

patient advocate: person who advocates (pleads for) for a patient; often family members and friends

phlebotomist: technician who draws blood

potentiation: synergistic effect, in which the effect of two drugs given simultaneously is greater than the effect of either drug given separately (Sell et. al.)

Pranic healing: a type of alternative healing method developed by Grandmaster Choa Kok Sui that utilizes prana to balance and transform energy. Prana is a Sanskrit term for "life forces." For more information: http://pranichealing.com/what-pranic-healing

primary caregiver: principle caregiver (typically non-medical) in a person's care

primary hospital: hospital that patient frequents; home hospital

R

radiation therapy: treatment of disease with radiation given off by special machines or radioactive isotopes (Sell et. al.)

rehabilitation: restoring a person to health and wholeness or normal functioning

Reiki: technique for stress reduction and relaxation that allows the patient to tap into an unlimited supply of "life force energy" to improve health and enhance the quality of life. Eastern medical theory suggests that humans are a mind-body-spirit unity and we are to live and act in a way that promotes harmony with others (Sell et. al.)

rheumatologist: physician that specializes in diseases associated with degeneration or inflammation of connective tissues (autoimmune disorders), e.g., scleroderma lupus, rheumatoid arthritis

S

scleroderma: autoimmune disease affecting the blood vessels and connective tissues. The skin becomes fixed to underlying tissue. There may be lung or heart complications leading to death (Sell et. al.)

Scleroderma Foundation: organization that supports individuals with scleroderma and their family/friends. For more information: http://www.scleroderma.org/site/PageServer

Shankar, Sri Sri Ravi: spiritual leader and founder of Art of Living Foundation, which teaches a breathing technique for self-healing. For more information: http://srisriravishankar.org/

singlehood: a category related to marital status in which one identifies as single

Sisters of St. Joseph of Carondelet: a group of sisters, originally from France who settled in St. Louis to work with deaf children. Founded a number of organizations, including Fontbonne University and the St. Joseph Institute for the Deaf. Established provinces in a number of states. Serves the dear neighbor worldwide and models unity and reconciliation. For more information: http://www.csjsl.org/

sociological imagination: a term coined by C. Wright Mills which refers to a deep understanding of the relationship between larger social forces and personal lives. Without employing the sociological imagination, we may fail to recognize the true origins and character of problems we face and may be unable to respond to them effectively (Lindsey, 2004)

sociopolitics: the underlying dynamics in social systems and interpersonal relationships; a combination of social and political factors. Example: the informal power structure in a hospital or corporation

Sui, Choa Kok: a spiritual leader who founded the energy medicine technique of Pranic Healing. For more information: http://www.pranichealing.org/

synergist: substance that augments the activity of another substance, agent, or organ, as one drug augmenting the effect of another. N. synergism, ADJ. synergistic. (Sell et. al.)

T

Tate, Billie Topa: a spiritual leader and healer who founded the Mystical Sciences Institute, which is an educational institution that promotes earth friendly endeavors. She is dedicated to the sacred principles of native cultures and has written books, lectured, and created effective meditation CDs, e.g., *Loving Kindness Meditation.* For more information: http://msi-healing.com/our-story/billie-topa-tate

Tessereau, Tom: a healer and teacher who owns and directs the Healing Arts Center, an educational institution that offers treatment and classes in a variety of energy/bodywork modalities, e.g., breathwork, Reiki, Pranic Healing, and massage. For more information: https://www.thehealingartscenter.com/

Tibetan Pulsing: Tibetan diagnostic procedure of pulsing, which emphasizes the mind-body connection. Process of inner transformation and healing which moves the client from mind to heart. For more information: http://www.tibetanpulsingworld.com/what-is.html

U

Usui Reiki: Dr. Mikao Usui, a Japanese Christian educator brought his Reiki principles based on ancient Buddhist teachings and written in Sanskrit to the United States. Addresses the body, mind and spirit and accelerates our ability to heal by redirecting the energy all around us into the client. For further information: https://www.thehealingartscenter.com/ or http://www.reiki.org/

W

Widowhood: the condition of being a widow/widower

References

Berger, Bennett M., ed. 1990. *Authors of Their Own Lives: Intellectual Autobiographies by Twenty American Sociologists*. Berkeley, CA: University of California Press.

Berger, Peter. 1963. *Invitation to Sociology*. New York: Bantam Doubleday Dell.

Brabant, Sarah. 1996. *Mending the Torn Fabric: For Those Who Grieve and Those Who Want to Help Them*. Amityville, NY: Baywood Publishing Co.

Brabant, Sarah. Fall 2006. "Metaphors as Tools in Clinical Sociology: Bereavement Education and Counseling." *Journal of Applied Sociology/Sociological Practice,* 23(2): 78-91.

Bradby, Hannah. 2009. *Medical Sociology: An Introduction*. London: SAGE Publications Ltd.

Chelsom, Peter. Dir. 2004. *Shall We Dance*. DVD. Santa Monica: Miramax Films.

Chopra, Deepak. 1994. *Seven Spiritual Laws of Success: A Practical Guide to the Fulfillment of Your Dreams*. Novato, CA: New World Library.

Dooley, Mike. "N. d". TUT. Notes from the Universe. Retrieved from www.tut.com.

Dorland, W. A. 2012. *Dorland's Illustrated Medical Dictionary*. 32nd ed. Philadelphia: Elsevier.

Duff, Raymond. 1987. "Close-up" versus "Distant" Ethics: Deciding the Care of Infants with Poor Prognosis. *Seminars in Perinatology* 11(3): 96.

Ebaugh, Helen. 1988. *Becoming an Ex: The Process of Role Exit*. Chicago and London: The University of Chicago Press.

Estess, Jenifer. 2004. *Tales from the Bed*. New York: Washington Square Press.

Fitzgerald, Sally., ed. 1979. *The Habit of Being: Letters of Flannery O'Connor*. New York: Farrar, Straus,and Giroux.

Franzoi, Stephen L. 2006. *Social Psychology*. 4th ed. New York: McGraw-Hill, Pp. 563-565.

Haigler, David H., Mims, Kathryn B., & Nottingham, Jack A. 1998. *Caring for You, Caring for Me: Education & Support for Caregivers, Participant's Manual*. Athens, GA: The University of Georgia Press.

Hay, Louise L. 1984. *Heal Your Body*. Carson, CA: Hay House, Inc.

Henslin, James M. 2014. *Sociology: A Down to Earth Approach*. 11th ed. Boston: Allyn and Bacon.

Lindsey, Linda and Beach, Stephen. 2004. Sociology. 3rd ed. Upper Saddle River, NJ: Pearson/Prentice Hall.

McCracken, Elizabeth. 2008. *An Exact Replica of a Figment of My Imagination*. New York: Little, Brown and Company.

Macionis, John J. 2014. *Sociology*. 15th ed. Upper Saddle River, New Jersey: Pearson/Prentice Hall.

Margolies, Luisa. 2004. *My Mother's Hip*. Philadelphia: Temple University Press.

Mills, C. W. 1959. *The Sociological Imagination.* London: Oxford University Press.

Neibuhr, Reinhold. 1944. *The Serenity Prayer* in the Federal Council of Churches.

Patterson, James. 2014. *Invisible*. New York: Little, Brown and Company.

Peabody, Francis. 1927. "*The Care of the Patient.*" *JAMA*: 1927; 88(12): 877-82.

Rapgay, Lopsang. 1996. *The Tibetan Book of Healing*. Salt Lake City: Morson Publishing.

Roth, Philip. 1996. *Patrimony*. New York: Vintage Books.

Ruiz, Don Miguel. 1997. *The Four Agreements: A Practical Guide to Personal Freedom*. San Rafael, CA: Amber-Allen Publishing.

Salva, Victor. Dir. 1995*. Powder*. DVD. Los Angeles: Buena Vista Pictures.

Scott, John and Marshall, Gordon. 2009. *Oxford Dictionary of Sociology*. 3rd rev. ed. London: Oxford University Press.

Sell, Rebecca, E., M.D., Rothenberg, Mikel. A., M.D., and Chapman, Charles F., M.D. 2013. *Dictionary of Medical Terms*. 6th ed. Hauppauge, NY: Barron's Education Series, Inc.

Shepard, Jon M. 2005. *Sociology*. 9th ed. USA: Wadsworth.

Sontag, Susan. 1978. *Illness As Metaphor*. New York: Anchor Books.

Steele, Stephen F. and Price, Jammie. 2004. *Applied Sociology: Terms, Topics, Tools, and Tasks*. Canada: Wadsworth.

Weitz, Rose. 2007. *The Sociology of Health, Illness, and Health Care*. 4th ed. Belmont, CA: Thomson Wadsworth.

Wise, Terry L. 2003. *Waking Up: Climbing Through the Darkness*. Oxnard, CA: Pathfinder Publishing of California.

Zucker, Jerry. Dir. 1990. *Ghost*. DVD. Los Angeles: Paramount Pictures.

Acknowledgments

Countless people helped me along the way in my healing journey and in the completion of this memoir. To each, I thank you.

My siblings and extended family members (nieces, nephews, and cousins) for their steadfast love and support on this project. My stepchildren, Angie, Mandy, and Peggy, for their ongoing support and unconditional acceptance of me. My aunt, Betty Schneider, as a great role model of grace and strength. May she rest in peace. Frank's extended family members for continuing to include me in family gatherings.

Penny Holste for her friendship and support since Frank's death and for her inspirational funeral program and message.

Cindy Goodnetter, Deb Hall, Pat Jordan, and Shari Liess for their generosity sharing alternative healing on spiritual, physical, and emotional planes; these colleagues and friends served as role models for my spiritual development and helped tremendously in my grief process.

Malinda Christ (Betty Crocker), a widow friend, who supported me in numerous ways in my grief. Mary Mondello and the other members of my Ignatian Prayer Group for their generosity and spiritual insights. Jack and Nan Sisk, owners of the Living Insight Center for healing and inspiration. Sue Brunner, Judy Hemker, Judy O'Leary, and Linda Whitman, good friends from my high school volleyball team, who gave me their fellowship and support over lunch and dinner for the last decade.

Cheryl Sklar, a dear friend, for her unconditional love and support and her editing contribution to this memoir. Becki Hafner for modeling empowerment and inspiring me to move forward in widowhood with her spirited and passionate hold on life. Eddie Hafner for his friendship and insight into the caregiving role. Marjorie Hafner for her encouragement and prayers. She was a loving spirit and angel among us. May she rest in peace. Ed Twesten for his companionship and compelling faith in the divine.

Doxey Sheldon, a sister in widowhood, for touching me with her grace and natural helpfulness.

My pastor and the other members of the parish council for giving me a strong sense of community.

The Sisters of St. Joseph of Carondelet and my fellow associates for sharing their boundless wisdom and spiritual gifts.

Suzanne Stoelting, a sociologist formerly at my university, for her inspiration and comforting humor. Daryl Wennemann, my colleague across the hall, for reading an early draft and giving me encouragement to write this story. Kevin Eiler for his compassion, patience, and extensive contributions to this work. Kristen Norwood for her generous and supportive spirit. Corinne Taff, Lisa Oliverio, and the other faculty colleagues located on my floor for their interest in this project. Jane Bidleman and Sue Ebenreck for their unconditional emotional support. Leslie Doyle, Sharon Jackson, Linda Maurer, Mazie Moore,

Frank's Arms: Acknowledgments

Beth Newton, Gale Rice, and Cat Connor-Talasek for their friendship and support in my grief. Members of the Information Technology department for responding graciously to my questions, especially Julianne Hayes. Mark Douglas for feedback on the artwork for the cover. Jane Theissen for copyright information. Teresa Sweeney for direction on the references section. The other countless co-workers and friends at my university who responded enthusiastically to this project and supported me in the process, particularly my departmental members.

Nancy Blattner, my friend and former Vice President of Academic Affairs at Fontbonne University for her support and loving presence during Frank's illness and my grieving process.

Randy Rosenberg for his friendship and encouragement to continue with this work. Ross Koppel and my wonderful colleagues and friends in the Association for Applied and Clinical Sociology who gave me suggestions in the earliest versions of this manuscript and enthusiastic support in the process. Michael Fleischer, Linda Lindsey, and Tina Quartaroli for their friendship and review of an early version of the memoir.

Kathleen Finneran, the instructor of the Creative Non-fiction writing course at Washington University Summer Writer's Institute, for her encouragement to write this memoir and her generosity in reviewing my final manuscript. The members of her class for suggestions on the assignments related to the memoir.

Jill and Ken Iscol for putting the fire in my creative engine.

My writers' group. Carolyn Carrera for her priceless support and encouragement; Tania Massamiri for her insight and wisdom in the early stages of this work; Lynne Klippel for her publishing tips; and Karen Coulson for her early ideas and editorial role in the completion of this memoir.

Patricia Feeney, my editor, for structure/content recommendations and her suggestions in the final edits of the manuscript. Rob Saigh for his editorial assistance. Cathy Wood for coaching me in the publishing process. Amanda Boatman for lending me the physical artwork for the cover and artist, Kurt Perschke, for granting me permission to use it.

About the Author

Deborah Phelps was born and raised in St. Louis, Missouri. She worked for a St. Louis construction company and the New York Stock Exchange before pursuing an undergraduate education as a non-traditional student at Washington University in St. Louis.

After obtaining a certificate in Health and Human Services and a degree in sociology, she completed two masters and a doctoral degree in medical sociology and social psychiatry from Yale University with a National Institutes of Health (NIH) pre-doctoral fellowship. In post-graduate academic studies, she earned a master's degree in psychiatric epidemiology and biostatistics from Washington University's School of Medicine as a post-doctoral fellow with the NIH. She also gained certification as a sociological practitioner from the Association for Applied and Clinical Sociology.

Deborah completed her training as an Usui Reiki Master, Integrated Breath worker, and Karuna Reiki practitioner with Tom Tessereau at the Healing Arts Center. She took classes in Rebirthing with Nancy Albertson, Synergy with Cynde Meyer, and the Sudarshan Kriya breathing technique with the St. Louis Art of Living Foundation. Her experiences in Pranic Healing, Esoteric Feng Shui, and Kriyashakti came from Grandmaster Choa Kok Sui and Master Stephen Co of the American Institute of

Asian Studies. She is a CranioSacral and Somatoemotional Release Therapy practitioner with the Upledger Institute, Inc. Finally, she is a licensed massage therapist based on her studies with Cindy Goodnetter at A Gathering Place Wellness Education Center.

Deborah is a professor of sociology at Fontbonne University and is on the editorial board of the *Journal of Applied Social Science*. In addition, she is an associate with the Sisters of St. Joseph of Carondelet and chair of her parish council.

She loves traveling, reading, theater, and spending time with her cat, Powder.